Collins

Incredible Earth 1

Meenakshi Atal
Debahuti Das

Components of DigiSuite

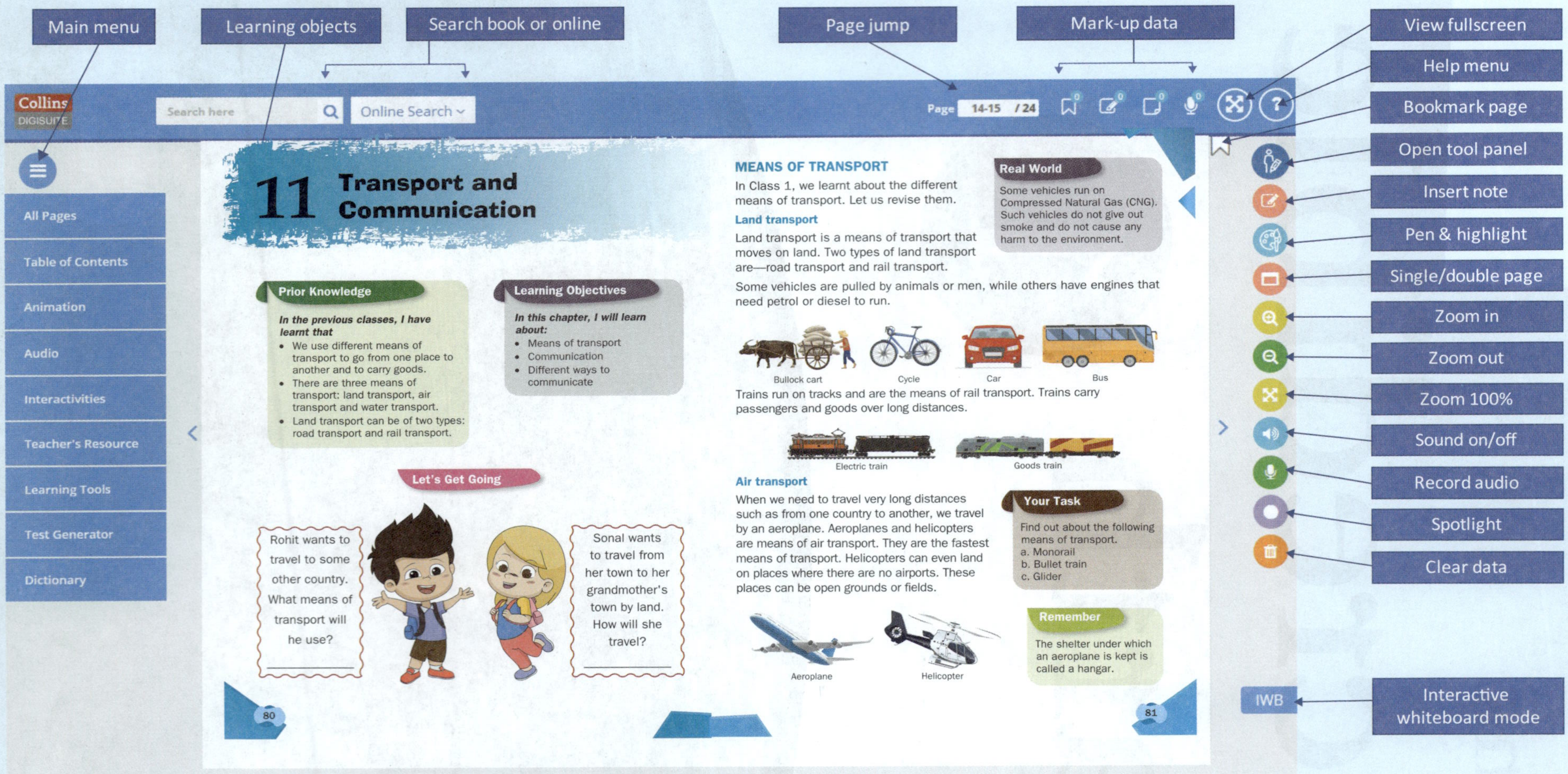

Student + Teacher			Teacher-only	
animations	ia activities	g games	lp lesson plans	tn teacher's notes
ilt instructor-led tutorials	w worksheets	v videos	w worksheets	ak answer keys
	audio			

Preface

Collins *Incredible* is a series of eight books for Classes 1 to 8. **Collins *Incredible Earth 1 and 2*** have been designed considering the multidisciplinary nature of Environmental Studies. **Collins *Incredible Science 3 to 8*** are focused on developing scientific skills and their application in real life.

This series adheres to the guidelines of the *National Education Policy (NEP) 2020* and aligns with the vision of the *National Initiative for Proficiency in Reading with Understanding and Numeracy* (NIPUN Bharat). It adopts the *5E Learning Model* and follows a thematic, coherent and structured approach, effectively integrating subject knowledge, NEP elements such as Experiential Learning, Art Integration, Cross-Curricular and India Focus and *21st Century Skills* for the overall development of the students. The series also aims to make the students aware of the *Sustainable Development Goals* (SDGs) of the United Nations so that they can become SDG Pioneers, Champions or Ambassadors.

SAFAL in **Collins *Incredible Series*:** This series also strives to make a shift from rote-learning to competency-based learning, in accordance with Structured Assessment For Analyzing Learning (SAFAL). The components of SAFAL—critical thinking, inquiry-based learning and analysis-based learning—are woven into the features such as Skills Enrichment Zone, Worksheets, the latest National Science Olympiad Paper, SEE Learning, Earth/Science Fair and Khagol Talim (Astronomy Education) Worksheets.

We would like to take this opportunity to thank all the teachers who reviewed the books and provided their invaluable feedback.
Any suggestions or constructive criticism from the users are welcome. We shall try to incorporate those in future editions.

Authors

About the Authors

Meenakshi Atal, former Vice Principal of The Heritage School, Kolkata, is an eminent educationist and teacher trainer with over four decades of experience.

Debahuti Das of The Heritage School, Kolkata, has a teaching career extending over two decades and has been a pioneer in evolving innovative methods of teaching.

Key Features

The key features of **Collins Incredible Series** are completely aligned with the *National Education Policy (NEP) 2020* and the vision of the *National Initiative for Proficiency in Reading with Understanding and Numeracy* (NIPUN Bharat). These meticulously designed features, based on the *5E Learning Model*, can be used as learning strategies to help in the overall development of scientific and *21st Century Skills* in students. These key features also aim to help the learners shift from rote-learning to competency-based learning, in accordance with *Structured Assessment For Analyzing Learning* (SAFAL).

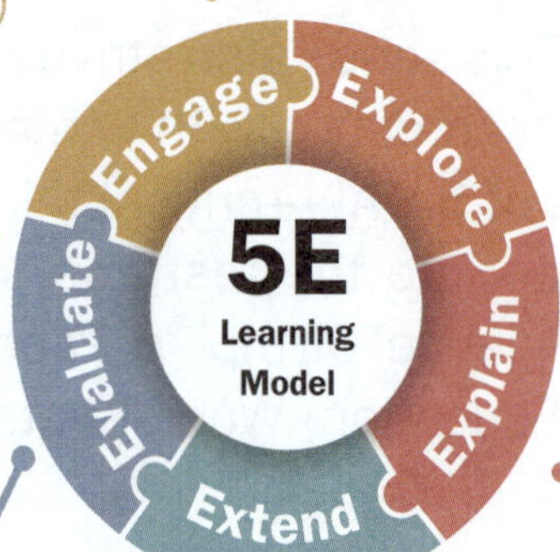

To capture the attention of students, get them mentally engaged and make connections between past and present

- I Am a Scientist! (Classes 3 to 8)
- Prior knowledge
- Let's Get Going
- Real World
- Science in Action (Classes 3 to 8)
- Concept Map
- Eminent Personalities/Scientists
- Picture Story

To enable the students to explore the concepts through hands-on activities, investigations, etc.

- Nature Trail/Science Around Us
- Let's Investigate (Classes 6 to 8)
- Tech Updates (Classes 3 to 8)
- Talk About (Classes 1 to 5)
- Your Task
- Let's Try
- SEE Learning
- Earth/Science Fair

To enable the students to understand the main ideas of the topics

- Learning Objectives
- Remember
- My Dictionary
- Summary
- Keywords (Classes 3 to 8)

To review, assess and evaluate what students have learned

- Knowledge Check
- Practice Zone
- Review Corner

To enable the students to stimulate thinking and apply prior and current knowledge to real-life situations

- Skills Enrichment Zone
- Worksheets

Adherence to National Education Policy

21st Century Skills (21 CS)

Learning Skills

- Critical Thinking
- Creativity and Innovation
- Collaboration
- Communication

Life Skills

- Flexibility and Adaptability
- Leadership and Responsibility
- Initiative and Self-Direction
- Productivity and Accountability
- Social and Cross-Cultural Interaction

Literacy Skills

- Information Literacy
- Media Literacy
- Technology Literacy

Art Integration (AI)

Cross Curricular (CC)

India Focus (IF)

Happiness Quotient (HQ)

Experiential Learning (EL)

SUSTAINABLE DEVELOPMENT GOALS

Each feature has been tagged with colour-coded icons to easily identify the type of skills and learning being addressed!

About the Features

To connect environmental studies/science with Indian history, art, culture and real-life situations

Selective topics that would serve as the basics to becoming a scientist

Interesting project ideas and thought-provoking questions to address the main elements of NEP 2020

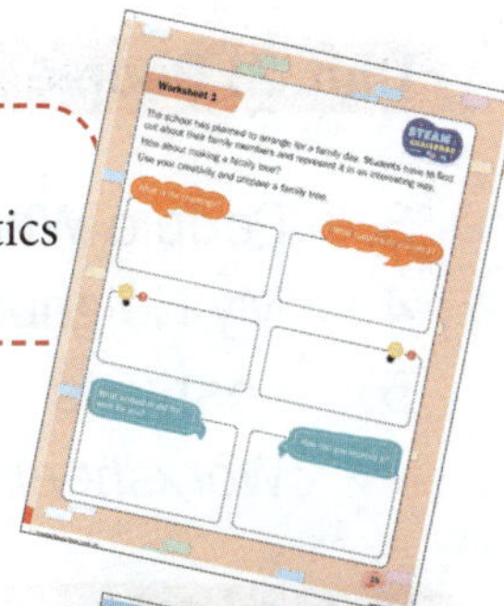

Interesting project ideas integrating Science, Technology, Engineering, Arts and Mathematics to solve real-world problems

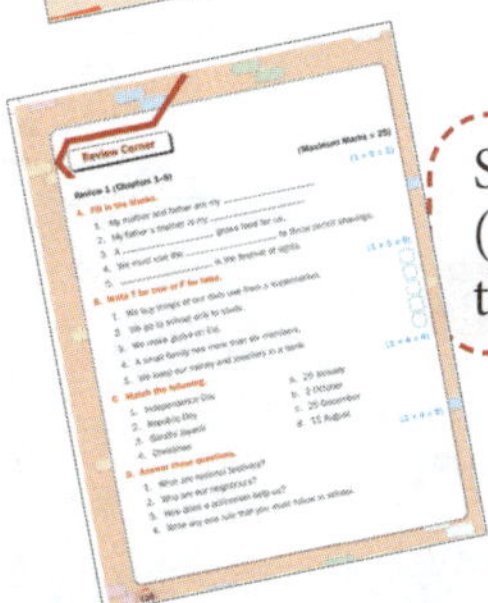

Sample test papers for review and assessment (Classes 6 to 8 Assessment Corner based on the **New Assessment format)**

Colourful cartoon spreads based on environmental awareness

Special stories to promote social, emotional and ethical learning

Innovative projects and model-making ideas that can be displayed in various school events

Brief write-up on the contributions of a few eminent personalities/ scientists

Informative and interactive colourful posters to focus on some important concepts or facts

Contents

Nature Trail

Folk Art Forms in India

21 CS Creativity and Innovation IF

Look at the pictures given below. You will see that these pictures talk about nature and our lives. Natural colours and ash, rice flour and fresh flower petals were used to make various folk arts as these are environment friendly.

Warli art from Maharashtra

Kolam art from Tamil Nadu

Madhubani art from Bihar

Which folk art form is famous in your area? Ask your elders and find out about more art forms famous in India.

With the help of an elder, collect some pictures of different folk art forms used in different parts of India and paste them in the space provided below.

Who Am I?

Hi!
My name is
________________.
I am ________ years old.
I am a ________ (boy/girl).

Paste a picture of yourself here.

My picture

My birthday is on
____
____
____

In my free time, I like to
____
____
____________________.

We all like to do different activities such as colouring, reading, playing and dancing in our free time.

We all have different likes and dislikes. The things we like the most are our **favourite** things.

These are a few of my favourite things.

My favourite colour: ____________________

My favourite book: ____________________

My favourite food: ____________________

My favourite game: ____________________

My favourite flower: ____________________

My favourite animal: ____________________

My Timeline

Paste your pictures here.

LET US SAY A PRAYER

Thank you God for making me 'Me',
I am someone no one can be!
Help me God to be always good,
And to do things which I should!
Keep me healthy, safe and chirpy,
Smiling, laughing and always happy!

1 My Family

Prior Knowledge

In the previous classes, I have learnt that

- We have a family.
- The family members care for each other and help one another.
- We have fun with our family.

Learning Objectives

In this chapter, I will learn about:

- Members of a family
- Small and big families

Let's Get Going

This is Rihaan's family.

Rihaan lives with his mother, father and sister.

His father's name is Sameer. He works in an office.

His mother's name is Aliya. She is a **homemaker**.

His sister's name is Samara. She goes to the same school as him. They are a happy family.

My Dictionary

homemaker: a person who takes care of the home and family

MEMBERS OF A FAMILY

Father, mother and children make a **family**. Our mother and father are called our **parents**. They look after us. Our sisters and brothers are called our **siblings**. They play with us.

Let's Try

My Family

Draw or paste a picture of your family here.

- I live with my ....
- There are .... members in my family.

SMALL AND BIG FAMILIES

Some families are **small**. Small families have father, mother and one child or two children.

Some families are **big**. Big families have father, mother, two or more children and grandparents.

Small family

Big family

Remember

A small family has not more than four members. Some small families may have only one parent (either father or mother) and one child or two children.

- Your father's or mother's parents are your **grandparents**. Your father's or mother's father is your **grandfather**. Your father's or mother's mother is your **grandmother**. You are their grandchild (**granddaughter** or **grandson**). A big family may also have other members such as uncles, aunts and their children.
- Your father's or mother's brother is your **uncle**.
- Your father's or mother's sister is your **aunt**.
- Your uncle's or aunt's children are your **cousins.**

The members of a family have fun together. They respect and help each other.

Real World

We have fun and share our happiness with our family on special days such as birthdays and festivals.

Talk About

- What do you do as a family in your holidays?
- What do you call your father's parents in your mother tongue?

Knowledge Check

Fill in the blanks.

1. Your father's sister is your ______________________.
2. Your uncle's children are your______________________ .
3. The members of a family have ________________together.

Concept Map

Family

- Small family
  - Father, mother and child/children
- Big family
  - Father, mother, children, grandparents, uncles, aunts, cousins

We care, we help, we love and we respect all the members of our family.

Summary

a. In this chapter, I have learnt that

- Father, mother and child/children make a family.
- Some families are small, while some are big.
- The members of a family respect and help each other.

b. I can do the following:

- Help my family members
- Share things with my family members
- Respect my family members

Practice ZONE

A. Match the following.

1.	Father's sister	a.	Cousins
2.	Mother's mother	b.	Aunt
3.	Uncle's children	c.	Grandmother

B. Write T for true or F for false.

1. Sonu has six members in his family. So, his family is small. ☐
2. Your mother and father are your parents. ☐
3. Your father's brother is your uncle. ☐

C. Give reasons for each of these.

1. Sometimes children live with only one parent, either mother or father, but they are a family.

____

2. Not only parents but children can also take care of their parents.

____

D. Answer these questions.

1. Who all are there in a small family?

____

2. How can a family have fun together?

____

E. Picture Talk

Draw two pictures of your favourite family activities. Name the activities.

______________________________ ______________________________

F. Out of the box!

A family of four lived in a two-room flat. Sonu and his sister shared a room. When Sonu got married, he moved to another house. Why do you think he did this?

____

____

Skills Enrichment ZONE

A. 21 CS Creativity and Innovation, Collaboration | AI | EL | HQ Harmony in Relationships

Peas in the Pod

1. Take a paper plate and colour it green.
2. Fold it in half.
3. Cut out circles of different sizes from a green chart paper with the help of an elder.
4. Draw the faces of the members of your family. Draw two little big ones for father and mother, and smaller ones for you and your sister or brother. Put these faces inside the folded part of the paper plate.

B. 21 CS Communication, Life Skills | CC Integration with English | HQ Living in an Interconnected Society

Interview a friend to find out about his or her family and make a diary entry.

Name of your friend: ____________________

Questions	Answers
How many members are there in your family?	
Who are they?	
What does your family do on a Sunday?	
Do you all go out for picnics?	
Do you have grandparents?	
If yes, how old are they?	

C. 21 CS Collaboration, Life Skills | CC Integration with English | HQ Cooperation and Collaborative Living

A family that prays together, stays together. So, let us say a prayer.

Dear God, look after my family,
Keep them safe and keep them happy.
In times of joy and in times of sorrow,
Keep us together in the years to follow!

D. 21 CS Critical Thinking, Life Skills | HQ Understanding Values in Relationships

Sharing is caring!
Your mother is not feeling well and your little sister is crying. What should you do? Tick the correct answer.

1. Go out to play ☐
2. Take care of your mother and sister ☐

E. 21 CS Collaboration, Life Skills

5 GENDER EQUALITY

Everyone in Shahid's family helps each other. Shahid and his father help in cleaning the house. His sister helps in washing the utensils. Shahid also helps in putting away things at their proper place.
Do you help out your family? Make a list of activities you help out in.

2 My School

Prior Knowledge

In the previous classes, I have learnt that

- We go to school to learn and to play with our friends.
- Teachers take care of us in school.

Learning Objectives

In this chapter, I will learn about:

- Going to school
- Things we learn in school
- Different sections of a school
- School rules
- Making friends and playing together

Let's Get Going

Draw or paste a picture of your school here.

The name of my school is ______________________.

I study in class ______________________.

GOING TO SCHOOL

We wear a uniform to school.

A school is a place to learn and play.
We make friends in school.
We wear a **uniform** when we go to school. Different schools have different uniforms. The uniform makes us look smart. It also makes us feel that we belong to a group, which is our school.
We carry a school bag when we go to school. We keep books, a pencil box, crayons, a ruler, a diary and a lunch box in our school bag.

Knowledge Check

Tick the items that you carry to school in your school bag.

 ◯  ◯ 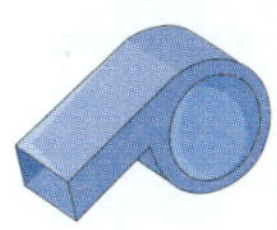 ◯ 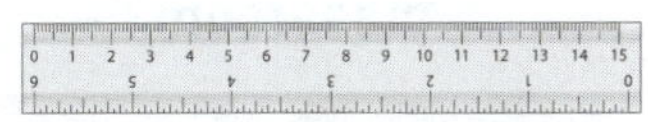 ◯

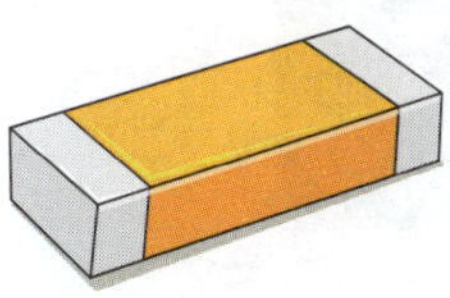 ◯  ◯  ◯

In school

Just like our parents take care of us at home, our **teachers** take care of us in the school. They teach us many things. We should respect our teachers.
The **principal** is the head of a school.

Real World

In the year 2020, as the world was affected by a virus called COVID-19, children had to stay home and attend online classes.

THINGS WE LEARN IN SCHOOL

In school, we learn to **read**, **write** and **count**.

We learn good **habits** and **manners**.

We learn to make friends and **share** our things with others. We also learn to **draw**, **paint**, **sing**, **dance** and **play** together.

Talk About

- How do you go to school?
- What do you like to do the most in school?

DIFFERENT SECTIONS OF A SCHOOL

A good school has the following sections.

We study in the **classroom**.

We read books in the **library**.

We learn about computers in the **computer lab**.

We play in the **playground**.

We have school functions in the **auditorium** or **hall**.

We learn music in the **music room**.

We go to the **sick (medical) room** when we get hurt or fall sick.

SCHOOL RULES

We must follow the school rules.

- Keep your classroom and school clean.
- Use the dustbin to throw pencil shavings and other waste.
- Greet your teachers in school.

Keep your classroom clean.

Use the dustbin to throw pencil shavings and other waste.

MAKING FRIENDS AND PLAYING TOGETHER

We go to school to make friends and learn together. It is fun to study and play together. We should always keep in mind the following things while making friends and playing with them.

- We must learn to share and care.
- We must be polite to our friends.
- We must look after and help one another.
- We must not fight with one another.

Talk About

How do you show that you care for your friends in school?

Children sharing lunch

A boy helping his schoolmate to get up

Concept Map

School

In school, we learn to:
- read, write and count
- good habits and manners
- make friends and share things with others
- draw, paint, sing, dance and play

The principal and teachers take care of us in school.

- We wear a uniform to school.
- We carry a school bag to school.
- We keep books, notebooks, pencil box and lunch box in our bag.

Summary

a. In this chapter, I have learnt that

- A school is a place to learn and play.
- We wear a uniform and carry a school bag when we go to school.
- The principal is the head of a school.
- A school has different sections such as classrooms, a library, a playground, an auditorium, a computer lab and a sick (medical) room.
- We must follow school rules.

b. I can do the following:

- Make friends and play with them in school
- Learn to read and write in school
- Share and care
- Learn to be polite

Practice ZONE

A. Fill in the blanks using the words given in the box.

principal	clean	different	auditorium	pencil box

1. Different schools have ________________ uniforms.
2. We keep a ________________ in the school bag.
3. The ________________ is the head of a school.
4. We have school functions in the ________________.
5. We should keep our classroom and school ________________ .

B. Match the following.

1.	We study in the	a.	computer room.
2.	We play in the	b.	music room.
3.	When we feel unwell in school, we go to the	c.	classroom.
4.	We learn music in the	d.	playground.
5.	We learn about computers in the	e.	medical room.

C. Give reasons for each of these.

1. All schools must have a sick room.

____

2. A school uniform is important.

____

D. Answer these questions.

1. Write any two things we learn in school.

____

2. Where do we read storybooks in school?

____

3. Write one rule that should be followed in school.

____

E. Picture Talk

Write four words to describe your teacher.

1. ______________________
2. ______________________
3. ______________________
4. ______________________

F. Out of the box!

Your friend is sick and could not make it to school today. How can you help him or her?

____

____

Skills Enrichment ZONE

A. 21 CS Critical Thinking AI

13 CLIMATE ACTION

Colour the dustbin given below and mention the items that we throw in our classroom dustbin.

1. ______________________
2. ______________________
3. ______________________
4. ______________________

B. 21 CS Critical Thinking, Life Skills HQ Cooperation and Collaborative Living

3 GOOD HEALTH AND WELL-BEING

Your classmate has broken his arm. How can you help him in school?

1. Help him to carry his bag ☐
2. Write his diary ☐
3. Play cricket with him ☐

Worksheet 1

STEAM CHALLENGE

The school has planned to arrange for a family day. Students have to find out about their family members and represent it in an interesting way.

How about making a family tree?

Use your creativity and prepare a family tree.

What is the challenge?

What supplies do you need?

1

2

What worked or did not work for you?

How can you improve it?

3 People Who Help Us

Prior Knowledge

In the previous classes, I have learnt that

- Many people help us in various ways.
- People work to help others.

Learning Objectives

In this chapter, I will learn about:

- People who help us in our daily lives and the work they do

Let's Get Going

Do you know how these people help us? Write a "Thank You" note to them.

Imagine what life would be like if we had nobody to help us—nobody to grow food, nobody to take care of us when we are sick, nobody to control traffic and nobody to fly aeroplanes or drive cars. So, it is important to have such people around us, as they make our lives easier and better.

PEOPLE WHO HELP US

A **teacher** teaches us.

A **fireman** puts out fire.

A **postman** brings us letters.

A **doctor** looks after us when we are sick.

A **cleaner** keeps our surroundings clean.

A **policeman** keeps us safe.

A **barber** cuts our hair.

A **carpenter** makes furniture for us.

A **shopkeeper** sells things we need.

A **driver** drives us around.

A **tailor** stitches our clothes.

A **farmer** grows food for us.

Talk About

Can you name two other people who help you in your daily life?

There are many other people who help us in our daily lives. These people work hard to make our lives better. We must respect and thank these people who make our lives comfortable.

Real World

People who help us in emergency situations are called emergency workers such as doctors, nurses, firemen, policemen and electricians.

Knowledge Check

Write T for true or F for false.

1. A farmer keeps us safe.
2. A doctor looks after us when we are sick.
3. A carpenter makes furniture for us.
4. A barber puts out fire.

Concept Map

Summary

a. In this chapter, I have learnt that

- There are many people who help us and make our lives easier and better.
- Farmer, teacher, policeman, postman, doctor, fireman, shopkeeper, carpenter, driver, cleaner and tailor are some of the people who help us.
- We must respect and thank people who make our lives comfortable.

b. I can do the following:

- Name different people who help us in our daily lives
- Respect and thank people who help us

Practice ZONE

A. Name the following.

1. A person who grows food for us ______________
2. A person who brings letters for us ______________
3. A person who makes furniture for us ______________
4. A person who stitches our clothes ______________
5. A person who sells the things we need ______________
6. A person who looks after us when we are sick ______________
7. A person who puts out fire ______________

B. Fill in the blanks using the words given in the box.

cleaner	teaches	barber

1. A ____________ cuts our hair.
2. A ____________ keeps our surroundings clean.
3. A teacher ____________ us.

C. Give reasons for each of these.

1. We need to thank the farmers before we eat our food.

____

2. We must respect a cleaner or a sweeper.

____

D. Answer these questions.

1. Name three people who help you in your daily life.

____

2. How does a policeman help you?

____

3. Who will you go to if you need to buy soap?

____

E. Picture Talk

Write two words to describe a policeman.

1. ____________________
2. ____________________

F. Out of the box!

Why do you think an ambulance turns on its siren as it rushes down the street?

____

____

Skills Enrichment ZONE

A. 21 CS Communication, Information Literacy | HQ Knowing My Needs

Find out and make a note of the following important telephone numbers.

1. Police station: ____________________
2. Fire station: ____________________
3. Nearest hospital: ____________________
4. My father's number: ____________________
5. My mother's number: ____________________

B. 21 CS Creativity and Innovation, Life Skills | AI | CC Integration with English | HQ Understanding Values in Relationships

Make two 'Thank you' cards for any two people who help you in your daily life.

C. 21 CS Critical Thinking, Life Skills | HQ Cooperation and Collaborative Living

3 GOOD HEALTH AND WELL-BEING

The school cleaner is unwell and is absent. How can you help to keep your classroom clean?

4 My Neighbours and Neighbourhood

Prior Knowledge

In the previous classes, I have learnt that

- Many people live around our house.
- Many important places are found near our house.

Learning Objectives

In this chapter, I will learn about:

- Neighbours
- What makes a good neighbourhood?

Let's Get Going

The Singh family has just moved into your neighbourhood. How can you help them settle down and feel happy? Discuss.

NEIGHBOURS

People who live near our house are our **neighbours**. Neighbours help each other and make good friends. Good neighbours do not fight with one another. Children living in a neighbourhood play together.

Your Task

- Find out the names of your next-door neighbours.
- Find out the name of a place where the following thing is found.

Let's Try

Take an interview of your next door neighbour.

Name: ____________________________

____

Number of family members: ____________

____

The work they do: ____________________

____

The language they speak: ______________

____

Do they have any pets? yes/no ____________________________

____

If yes, what kind of pet do they have? ____________________________

WHAT MAKES A GOOD NEIGHBOURHOOD?

The area around our house forms our **neighbourhood**. There are many important places that can be found in our neighbourhood. A good neighbourhood will have most of these places.

Talk About

How can neighbours help each other?

Places in the Neighbourhood

A **bank** is a place where we keep our money and jewellery for safety.

A **police station** is the place where policemen work. The police protects us from thieves and robbers, and keeps our neighbourhood safe.

When we are sick, we go to a **hospital**. The doctor does a check up and gives us medicines.

Post Office
A post office is a place from where we send letters and parcels.
Fire Station
A fire station is the place where firemen work. Firemen put out fire for us.
A park is a place where children play and adults walk, exercise or talk to their friends.
Supermarket
Cafe
We buy things for our daily use from the market or a supermarket.
STOP
School
A school is a place where children go to learn and play.

Knowledge Check

Name the following.

1. People who live near your house __________
2. A place where we keep our money and jewellery for safety __________
3. A place where we go when we are sick __________

Concept Map

Summary

a. In this chapter, I have learnt that

- People who live near our house are our neighbours.
- The area around our house forms our neighbourhood.

b. I can do the following:

- Be helpful to my neighbours
- Keep my neighbourhood clean
- Visit a park in my free time

Practice ZONE

A. Fill in the blanks using the words given in the box.

help	bank	neigbours

1. ________________ are people who live near our house.
2. Good neighbours ________________ each other.
3. A ________________ is a place where we keep our money for safety.

B. Write T for true or F for false.

1. We buy things of our daily use from a supermarket. ☐
2. A fire station helps us by sending doctors to put out fire. ☐
3. A park is a place where only children play. ☐

C. Give reasons for each of these.

1. It is important to have a hospital in the neighbourhood.

____

2. It is important to be friendly with our neighbours.

____

D. Answer these questions.

1. Who is a neighbour?

____

2. What is neighbourhood?

____

3. Name two places that a good neighbourhood should have.

____

4. Where do we go to learn and play?

____

E. Picture Talk

Mr Gill has just moved to a new area. Do you think he has a good neighbourhood? Give reasons for your answer.

____

____

F. Out of the box!

When the Sen family went on a holiday, they left the keys with their neighbour. Do you think it was a wise thing to do?

____

____

Skills Enrichment ZONE

A. 21 CS Critical Thinking, Information Literacy | CC Integration with Social Studies | HQ Living in an Interconnected Society

11 SUSTAINABLE CITIES AND COMMUNITIES

Look at the map and answer the following questions.

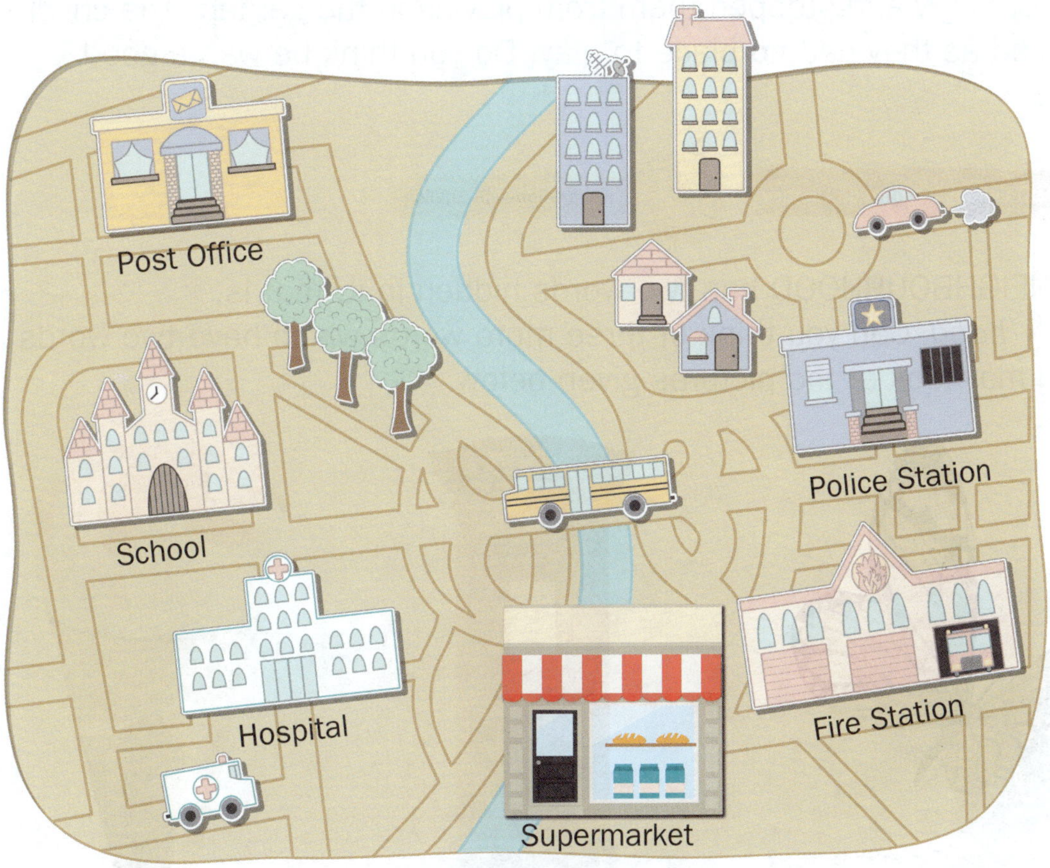

1. Name the place where we can go and buy things. ________________
2. Where do we go when we are sick? ________________
3. The thief was taken to a ________________ by the police.
4. Sara wants to send a parcel to her grandparents. Where does she go?
____
5. There was a fire next door. Where will you call for help?
____
6. Children go to ________________ to learn and to play.

B. 21 CS Critical Thinking, Life Skills | CC Integration with English | HQ Cooperation and Collaborative Living

Read the story and answer the question.

Once there lived a giant who had a big garden. In his neighbourhood, there lived a lot of children. They came to the garden and played happily. One day the giant got angry and stopped them from playing in the garden. The children were very sad as they had no place to play. Do you think he was a good neighbour?

C. 21 CS Critical Thinking, Information Literacy | CC Integration with English

The word NEIGHBOURHOOD has two words hidden in it, that is, *neighbour* + *hood*. Can you think of three more words which have two words in them? You may look at the pictures given below.

1 ____________ + ____________

2. ____________ + ____________

3. ____________ + ____________

5 Festivals

Prior Knowledge

In the previous classes, I have learnt that

- We have family and friends.
- Some days are special days.
- We should celebrate special days with them.

Learning Objectives

In this chapter, I will learn about:

- Fun with our family and friends
- Celebrating special days
- Religious festivals
- National festivals

Let's Get Going

Look at the picture and answer the question.

What is Dina celebrating? ______________

FUN WITH OUR FAMILY AND FRIENDS

We must have fun along with studies. That is why we need to have free time to do things that we enjoy. We have fun with our family and friends. Here are some of the ways to have fun with our family and friends.

Watching television

Going to a park

CELEBRATING SPECIAL DAYS

We celebrate special days with our family and friends. On these days, we decorate our house, make special food and enjoy the day with our family and friends.

FESTIVALS

India is a land of festivals. We celebrate two types of festivals. They are religious festivals and national festivals.

Religious festivals

Diwali

Diwali is the festival of lights. On this day, people decorate their houses by lighting diyas, candles or colourful lights. Many people wear new clothes and pray to god. They also give gifts and sweets to family and friends.

Diwali

Eid

On Eid, people go to the mosque and pray. They hug and wish each other 'Eid Mubarak'. People give gifts and sweets to one another. They also give money to the poor. People prepare a special sweet called *sewaiyan*.

Eid

Christmas

Christmas is celebrated on 25th December every year. It was on this day that Jesus Christ was born. People go to the church to pray. They decorate a Christmas tree in their homes and give gifts and sweets to each other. They also help the poor and the needy.

Christmas

Gurpurab

People celebrate Guru Nanak's birthday as Gurpurab. On this day, people go to the Gurdwara and pray, and offer food to the poor. They light up their houses and eat together.

Gurpurab

Holi

Holi is the festival of colours. We apply colours to each other's face.
Many people make a special sweet called *gujiya* on this day.

Holi

Knowledge Check

Match the following.

1. Eid	a. Festival of colours
2. Christmas	b. People eat *sewaiyan*
3. Holi	c. Jesus Christ's birthday

Real World

Kite festival is celebrated in India, China and Japan. People celebrate this festival by flying big, colourful kites.

National festivals

National festivals are celebrated by the people of a country. In India, we have three national festivals. These are Republic Day, Independence Day and Gandhi Jayanti.

Republic Day

Republic Day is celebrated on 26th January every year. It was on this day that the Rule Book of India was first presented to the people.

On Republic Day, a parade is held

On Independence Day, the national flag is hoisted at the Red Fort

Independence Day

Independence Day is celebrated on 15th August. On this day, India became a free country.

On Republic Day and Independence Day, people hoist the **national flag** and sing the **national anthem**.

Gandhi Jayanti

Gandhi Jayanti is celebrated on 2nd October. It is the birthday of Mahatma Gandhi who is also known as Bapu or the 'Father of the Nation'.

Mahatma Gandhi

Talk About

Which is your favourite festival? How do you celebrate it?

Your Task

Find out the difference between religious festivals and national festivals.

Concept Map

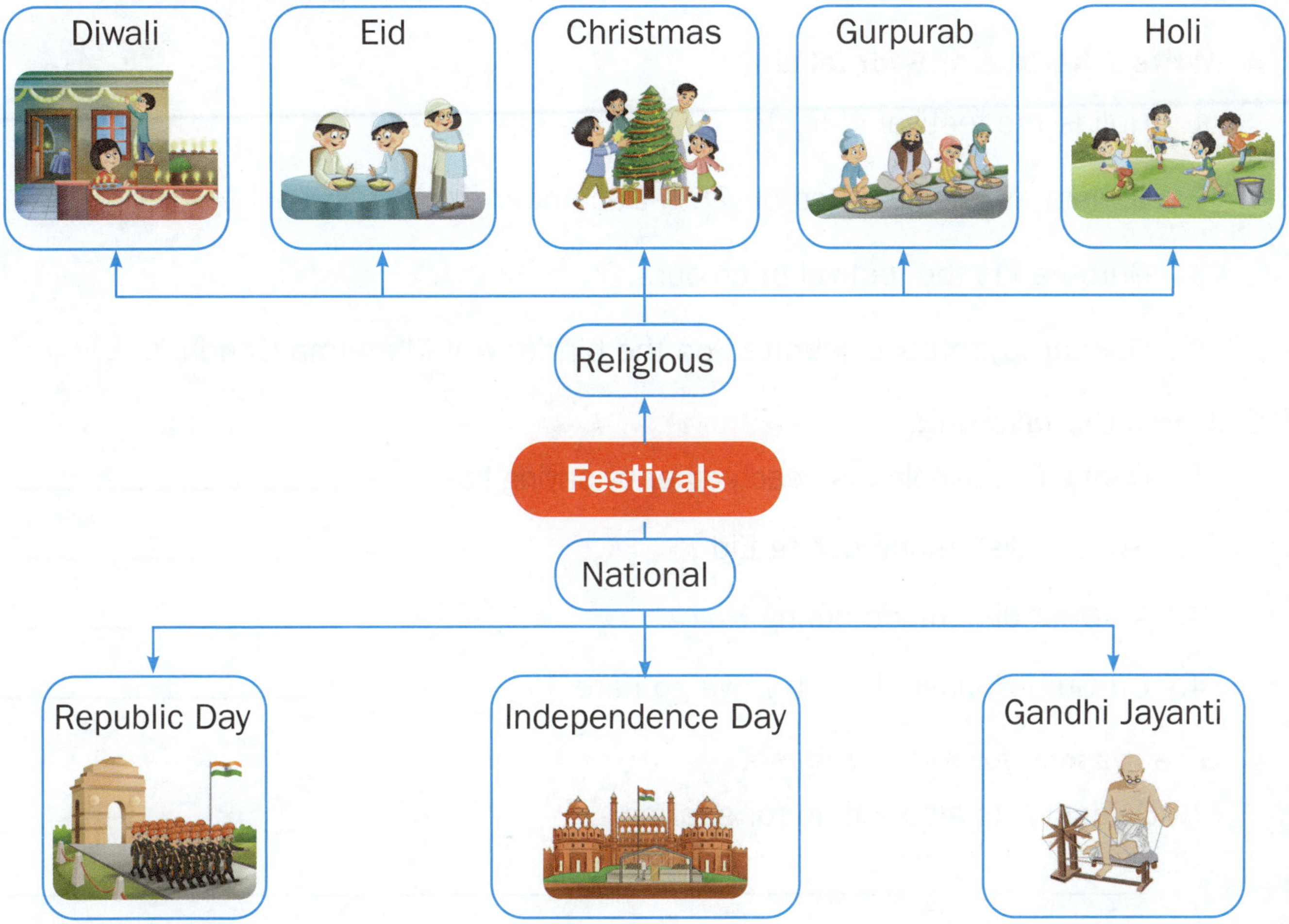

Summary

a. In this chapter, I have learnt that

- We celebrate special days with our family and friends.
- India is a land of festivals.
- There are two types of festivals—religious festivals and national festivals.

b. I can do the following:

- Have fun with my family members on special days
- Help my mother to decorate the house during festivals

Practice ZONE

A. Write T for true or F for false.

1. Holi is the festival of lights. ☐
2. Christmas is celebrated on 25th December every year. ☐
3. Gurpurab is the festival of colours. ☐
4. Gandhi Jayanti is celebrated on the birthday of Mahatma Gandhi. ☐

B. Name the following.

1. During Eid, people wish each other by saying this ____________
2. Special dish made during Eid ____________
3. A sweet dish made during Holi ____________
4. On Guru Nanak's birthday, we go here ____________

C. Give reasons for each of these.

1. A festival is also a time for sharing.

   ____

2. Festival is a time for happiness.

   ____

D. Answer these questions.

1. What are the two types of festivals?

   ____

2. Name three religious festivals.

   ____

3. How do we celebrate Christmas?

   ____

4. What special sweet do many people make on Holi?

   ____

E. Picture Talk

Identify the festivals and write their names in the space provided below.

1. ____________________ 2. ____________________

F. Out of the box!

All countries have a Rule Book. Why?

____

____

Skills Enrichment ZONE

A. 21 CS Creativity and Innovation, Life Skills | AI | EL | HQ Harmony in Relationships

Make a Christmas gift!

1. Take a small cardboard box.
2. Paste wrapping paper, ribbon strips and coloured tape on the top of the box. You can also use glitter to decorate the box.
3. Fill the box with sweets and candies.
4. Close the box with the help of a ribbon.
5. You may now gift it to someone on Christmas.

B. 21 CS Critical Thinking, Life Skills | HQ Coexisting with Nature

13 CLIMATE ACTION

Do not buy noisy and harmful crackers on Diwali. Buy only sparklers that do not give out thick, black smoke. This smoke creates trouble for all life forms. What else can you do to celebrate a green diwali?

Worksheet 2

STEAM CHALLENGE

It is your best friend's birthday. You want to make it special by creating something interesting with your hands.

What about making a party popper?

Use your creativity and make a fantastic party popper.

What is the challenge?

What supplies do you need?

IDEA 1

IDEA 2

What worked or did not work for you?

How can you improve it?

6 Living and Non-living Things

Prior Knowledge

In the previous classes, I have learnt that

- Things around us can be living or non-living.
- People, animals and plants are living things.
- Non-living things have no life.

Learning Objectives

In this chapter, I will learn about:

- What do living things do?
- What do non-living things do?

Let's Get Going

Look at the picture and write the names of three living and three non-living things that you can see.

Living things: ....

Non-living things: ....

Plants, animals and human beings are living things. Living things are different from non-living things. Let us discuss how.

Talk About

What makes you say that some things are living while others are non-living?

WHAT DO LIVING THINGS DO?

- Living things breathe.

Girl breathing

- Living things can move on their own.

Boy running

- Living things grow.

Baby boy grows into a man

Real World

A plant may not move from place to place but some of its parts show movement. For example, buds bloom into flowers.

- Living things eat.

Cow eating grass

- Living things can feel.

Wounded boy crying

- Living things **produce** babies.

Duck with ducklings

My Dictionary

produce: to make or create something

WHAT DO NON-LIVING THINGS DO?

A non-living thing cannot do what a living thing can do. Non-living things do not breathe, move on their own, grow, eat, feel and produce babies.

Your Task

Name an object that can move, talk and walk but is not a living thing.

Some examples of non-living things are eraser, table, bag and football.

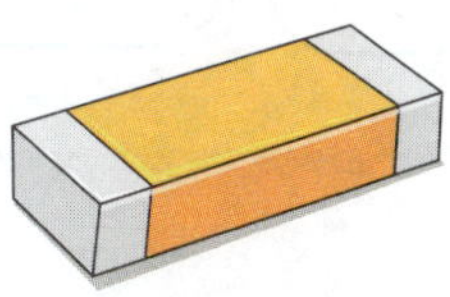

Eraser

Table

Bag

Football

Knowledge Check

Circle the pictures of living things.

Concept Map

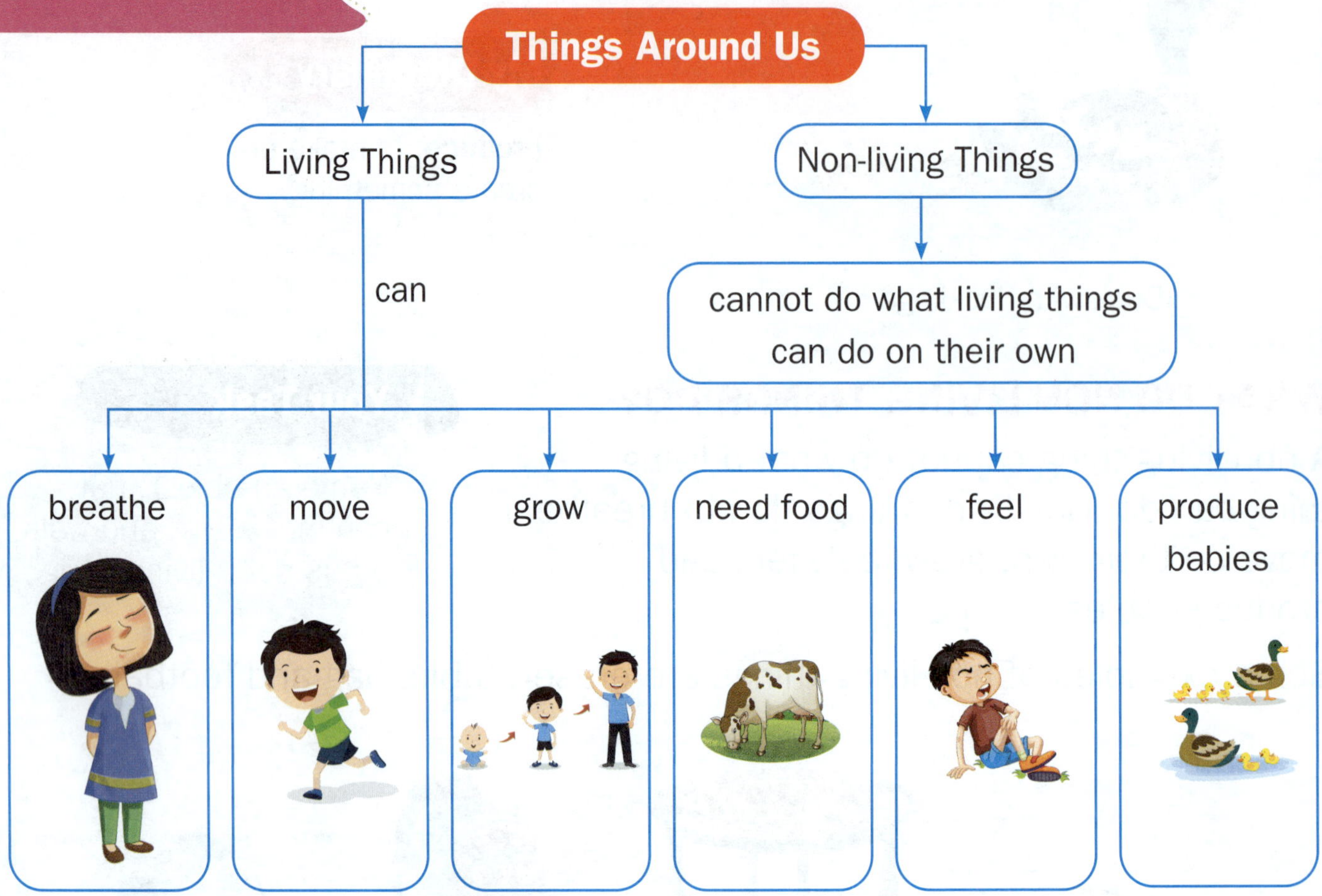

Summary

a. In this chapter, I have learnt that

- Plants, animals and human beings are living things.
- Living things breathe, move on their own, grow, eat, feel and produce babies.
- Non-living things cannot breathe, move on their own, grow, eat, feel and produce babies.

b. I can do the following:

- Tell what are living things and what are non-living things
- Tell that I am a living thing

Practice ZONE

A. Look at the pictures and identify the living and non-living things. Write their names in the given table.

Book

Bird

Bat

Blackboard

Tree

Girl

Living things	Non-living things

B. Fill in the blanks using the words given in the box.

grow   living   cat   cannot   non-living

1. Seema's doll is a ________________ thing.
2. A fish can ________________ in size.
3. A ________________ produces kittens.
4. A table ________________ move from place to place on its own.
5. ________________ things feel happiness and pain.

C. Give reasons for each of these.

1. A plant cannot move, yet it is a living thing.

____

2. A car can move, yet it is a non-living thing.

____

D. Answer these questions.

1. Name three things that a living thing can do.

____

2. How does a plant show movement?

____

3. Is a robot a living thing? Why or why not?

____

E. Picture Talk

How do we know whether the alarm clock is a living or a non-living thing?

- Does it breathe?
- Does it grow?
- Does it move?
- Does it eat food?
- Does it feel?
- Does it produce babies?

Is it a living or a non-living thing?

____

Why do you think so?

____

F. Out of the box!

What will happen if all the hens stop laying eggs?

____

____

Skills Enrichment ZONE

A. 21 CS Critical Thinking, Life Skills AI HQ How Similar are We

Collect photographs of your mother as a baby (less than one-year-old), as a ten-year-old, as a twenty-year-old and her picture now. Paste them in your scrapbook. How are these pictures different?

B. 21 CS Critical Thinking CC Integration with English HQ Coexisting with Nature

Rearrange the jumbled letters and tick the right answer to show whether they are living or non-living things.

1. EABTL ____________________ (living/non-living)
2. ILNO ____________________ (living/non-living)
3. EPEHS ____________________ (living/non-living)
4. RETE ____________________ (living/non-living)

C. 21 CS Critical Thinking CC Integration with English

Put the following words in alphabetical order.

1. deer, zebra, elephant, ant, parrot, owl

____

2. table, napkin, cup, fan, dress, spoon

____

D. 21 CS Critical Thinking

15 LIFE ON LAND

Which one do you think is more important: living things or non-living things? Give reasons for your answer.

7 Plants Around Us

Prior Knowledge

In the previous classes, I have learnt that

- There are many plants around us.
- We know the names of some plants.
- Most plants grow on land but some plants grow in water.

Learning Objectives

In this chapter, I will learn about:

- Big plants and small plants
- Different plants grow in different places
- Parts of a plant
- Taking care of plants

Let's Get Going

Go on a nature walk with your parents. Write the names of two big plants and two small plants that you see on your way.

____

____

BIG PLANTS AND SMALL PLANTS

There are different kinds of plants around us. Plants have different shapes and sizes. Very big plants are called trees. They are strong and tall. Trees have hard, woody stems called trunks. Neem and banyan are examples of trees.

Neem tree

Banyan tree

Real World

Banyan tree is the national tree of India.

Your Task

Some plants such as rose have thorns. What are thorns?

Some plants are much smaller than trees. Rose, *Hibiscus* and grass are examples of small plants.

Rose plant

Hibiscus plant

DIFFERENT PLANTS GROW IN DIFFERENT PLACES

- Some plants such as mango and neem grow in the **plains**.
- Some plants such as fir and pine grow in cold mountains or hills.
- Some plants such as lotus grow in water.

My Dictionary

plains: a large area of flat land

Lotus plant

Pine tree

PARTS OF A PLANT

Let us study the different parts of a plant.

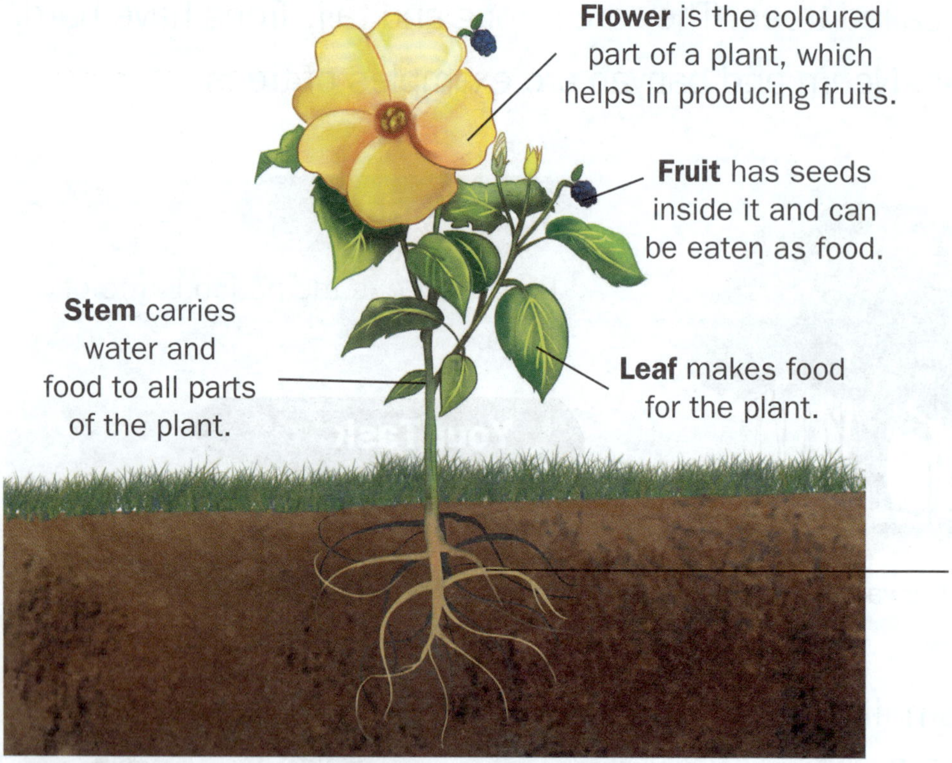

Parts of a plant

Real World

A seed has a baby plant inside it which grows into a new plant.

What does a plant need to grow?

A plant needs air, water, sunlight and soil to grow.

Knowledge Check

Fill in the blanks.

1. __________ and __________ plants grow in the plains.
2. __________ plant grows in water.
3. A plant needs __________, __________, __________ and __________ to grow.

How do plants help us?

Plants help us in many ways. Plants give us shade, clean air and fruits and vegetables as food.

Fruits and vegetables

TAKING CARE OF PLANTS

- We should take care of plants and trees.
- We must water them.
- We should not cut trees.

Water plants regularly

Concept Map

Plants Around Us

- Types of plants:
  - **Big Plants** such as banyan tree and neem tree
  - **Small Plants** such as rose, *Hibiscus*, and grass
- Plants need: air, water, sunlight and soil to grow
- Plants grow in:
  - the plains
  - old mountains and hills
  - water
- Parts of plants: flower, fruit, stem, leaf, root
- Plants give us: food, shade and fresh air
- Take care of plants by:
  - watering them
  - not cutting them

Summary

a. In this chapter, I have learnt that

- Plants have different shapes and sizes.
- Different plants grow in different places.
- Plants need air, water, sunlight and soil to grow.
- Plants give shade, clean air and food.

b. I can do the following:

- Name the different parts of a plant
- Grow plants and look after them

Practice ZONE

A. Fill in the blanks using the words given in the box.

big	water	mountains	trees	stems

1. Big plants are called ____________________.
2. Neem is a ____________________ plant.
3. Hard, woody ____________________ of trees are called trunks.
4. Lotus grows in ____________________ .
5. A pine tree grows in the ____________________ .

B. Find the names of eight plants given in the grid and circle them.

NEEM BANYAN MANGO ROSE HIBISCUS CACTUS FIR PINE

N	T	T	Z	L	C	K	V
B	F	C	P	T	A	N	O
H	I	B	I	S	C	U	S
C	D	S	N	S	T	C	Q
L	N	E	E	M	U	D	V
X	F	I	R	O	S	E	Q
E	B	A	N	Y	A	N	I
C	E	O	M	A	N	G	O

C. Give reasons for each of these.

1. Cutting of trees affect the birds.

____

2. Leaf of a plant is called its kitchen.

____

D. Answer these questions.

1. Where do plants grow?

____

2. What do plants need to grow?

____

3. What do plants give us?

____

E. Out of the box!

Which part of the rice plant do we eat?

____

F. Picture Talk

Join the numbered dots. Then colour the picture. What did you find?

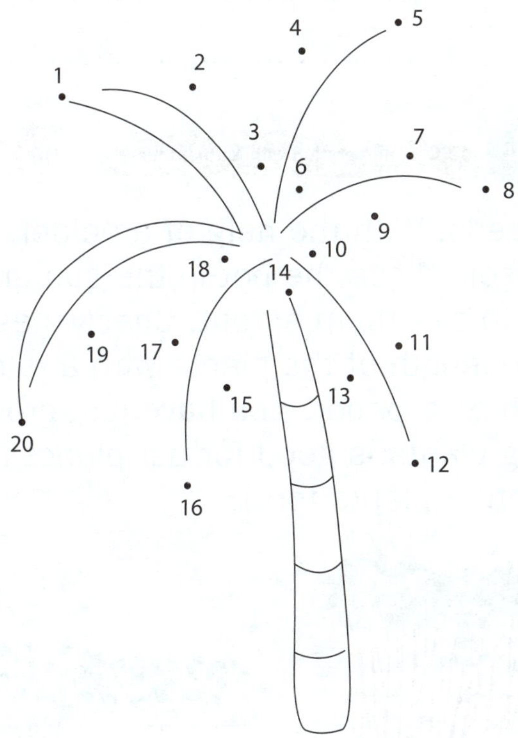

This is a ____________________ tree.

Skills Enrichment ZONE

A. 21 CS | Collaboration, Life Skills | AI | EL | HQ | Coexisting with Nature

15 LIFE ON LAND

Go for a walk with an elder and find out about different plants. Collect their leaves and dry them by keeping them under the folds of a newspaper. Once they are dry, paste them in your scrapbook and write the names of the plants they belong to.

B. 21 CS | Critical Thinking, Life Skills | HQ | Coexisting with Nature

Find out the uses of the following plants.

1. Neem ....
2. Rose ....
3. Coconut tree ....
4. Mint ....
5. Henna ....

C. 21 CS | Collaboration, Life Skills | EL | CC | Integration with Mathematics | HQ | Coexisting with Nature

15 LIFE ON LAND

Take some mustard seeds. With the help of an elder, put them in a big pot filled with soil. Place the pot in the sun and do not forget to water it daily to see them sprout. Check these plants every day. Measure the length of the plants with a ruler and keep a record of their growth on a paper. You have just grown some healthy plants! Growing plants is good for our planet Earth. (You can try this with other plants too.)

8 Animals Around Us

Prior Knowledge

In the previous classes, I have learnt that

- We see many animals, birds and insects around us.
- Some animals live in the forest while some animals live on farms or in our house.

Learning Objectives

In this chapter, I will learn about:

- Big animals and small animals
- Where do animals live?
- Wild animals
- Domestic animals
- Birds
- Insects

Let's Get Going

Hiyang went to the zoo with his grandfather. Write the names of five animals that he saw in the zoo.

1. ____________ 2. ____________ 3. ____________

4. ____________ 5. ____________

BIG ANIMALS AND SMALL ANIMALS

Animals are found all over the world. They are of different shapes, sizes and colours. Some animals are big and some are small.

Your Task

Which is the largest living animal?

Elephants, giraffes and rhinoceroses are examples of big animals.

Elephant

Giraffe

Talk About

Which is your favourite animal? What do you like about it?

Some animals such as rabbits, rats and squirrels are small.

Rabbit

Rat

WHERE DO ANIMALS LIVE?

Some animals such as deer, zebras, cows, camels and elephants live on land.

Deer

Zebra

Real World

Some animals such as flying squirrels and flying frogs can fly in the air.

Flying squirrel

Flying frog

Some animals such as monkeys and squirrels live on trees.

Monkey

Squirrel

Some animals such as fish, turtles and dolphins live in water.

Fish

Turtle

Dolphin

Some animals such as frogs, crocodiles and salamanders live both on land and in water.

Frog

Crocodile

Salamander

Knowledge Check

Name the following.

1. Two animals that live on land ______________, ______________
2. Two animals that live on trees ______________, ______________
3. Two animals that live in water ______________, ______________
4. Two animals that can live both on land and in water ______________, ______________

WILD ANIMALS

Animals that live in the forest are called **wild animals**. Some examples of wild animals are tigers, lions and bears.

Tiger

Bear

We may see some of these wild animals in the zoo.

Real World

Camels are known as the ship of the desert as they carry people and heavy things across the hot desert.

DOMESTIC ANIMALS

Animals that live in our homes or on farms are called **domestic animals**. Domestic animals that are kept on farms are called farm animals. Horses, donkeys, hens and cows are some examples of farm animals. Horses and donkeys are used to carry heavy things. Domestic animals that are kept at homes are called pet animals. Dogs and cats are examples of such animals.

A cow gives us milk.

A hen gives us eggs and meat.

A dog guards our house.

BIRDS

Birds are animals with feathers and beaks. They also have two legs which help them to walk or swim. They do not have teeth and they use their beaks to eat. Most birds fly in the air with the help of their wings. Some birds, such as ducks and swans, swim in water. Some birds, such as penguins, ostriches and emu, cannot fly.

Pigeon

Duck

Penguin

INSECTS

Insects are very small in size. They have three pairs of legs. Some have wings too. Fleas, lice, silverfish, and firebrats do not have wings.

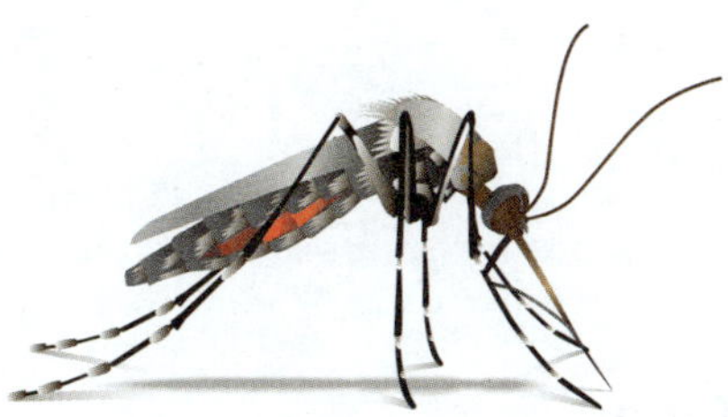
Mosquito

Cockroach

Louse

Talk About

How many insect names do you know?

Your Task

Find out the number of insects found on Earth.

Concept Map

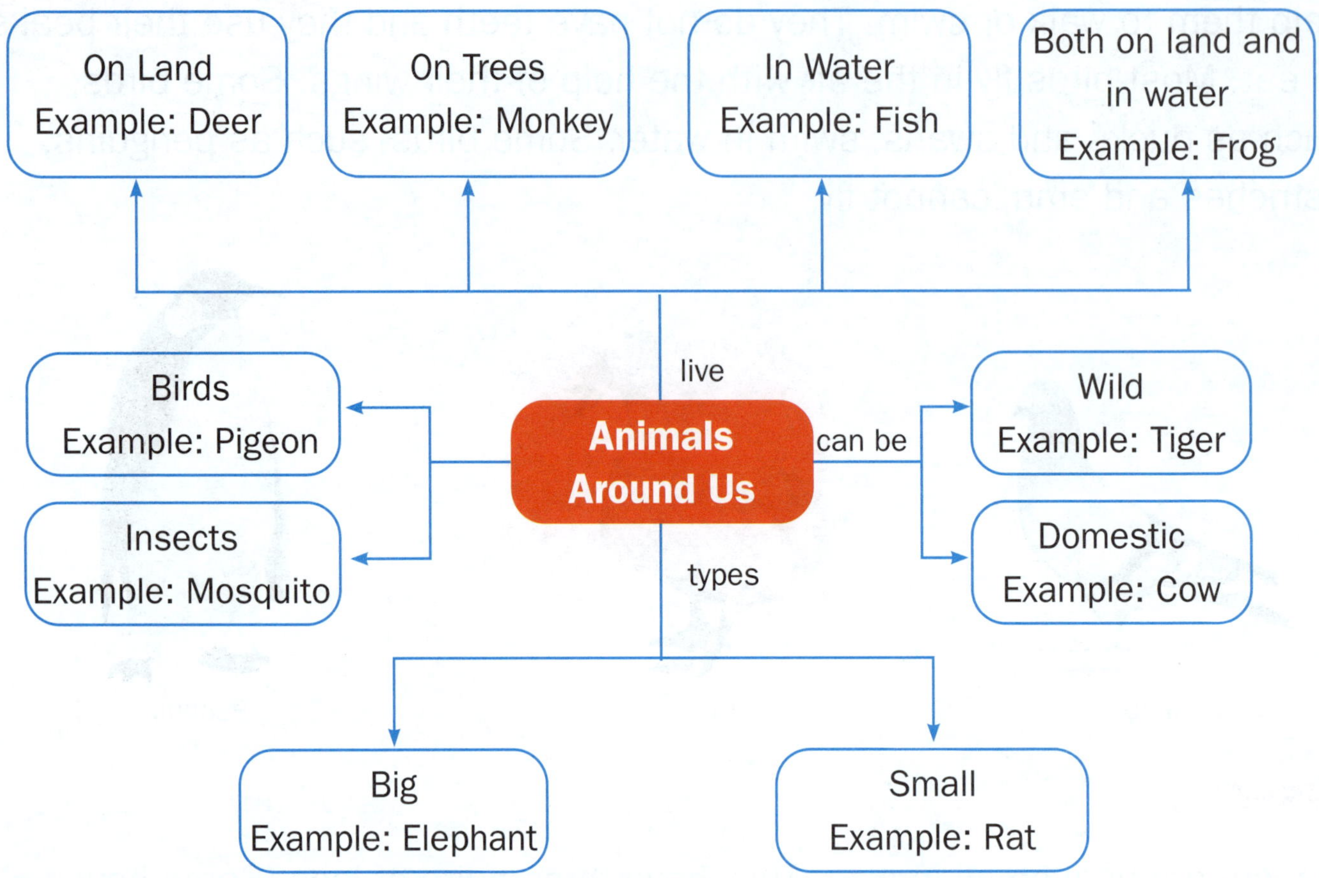

Summary

a. In this chapter, I have learnt that

- Animals live on land, trees and in water.
- Birds have wings, feathers and beaks.
- Insects are very small in size with three pairs of legs.

b. I can do the following:

- Name wild and domestic animals
- Name birds that can fly, birds that cannot fly and birds that can swim
- Identify insects

Practice ZONE

A. Fill in the blanks using the words given in the box.

salamander	hens	cow	big

1. A rhinoceros is a ________________ animal.
2. A ________________ lives both on land and in water.
3. We get milk from ________________ .
4. ________________ give us meat and eggs.

B. Write T for true or F for false.

1. A giraffe is a farm animal. ☐
2. Horses are used to carry heavy things. ☐
3. Birds eat with their beaks. ☐
4. An ostrich can fly with the help of wings. ☐

C. Give reasons for each of these.

1. Birds are different from all the other creatures.

____

2. We need to protect ourselves from mosquito bites.

____

D. Answer these questions.

1. Name two big animals.

____

2. What are pet animals?

____

3. Name any three insects.

____

E. Picture Talk

Which animal would you like to keep as a pet? Draw the animal. How will you look after it?

F. Out of the box!

Shankar is a farmer. He keeps oxen and bullocks on his farm. Why do you think he does that?

____

____

Skills Enrichment ZONE

A. 21 CS Critical Thinking, Life Skills | HQ Coexisting with Nature

Find the names of five wild and five domestic animals in the wordsearch. Circle the wild animals with green and the domestic animals with red.

TIGER ELEPHANT GIRAFFE COW HORSE
FOX DOG SHEEP LION BUFFALO

E	B	U	F	F	A	L	O
L	R	Y	R	S	Z	C	J
E	Q	A	H	P	F	O	X
P	V	L	O	V	N	W	R
H	G	I	R	A	F	F	E
A	J	K	S	H	E	E	P
N	L	W	E	S	J	Q	W
T	I	G	E	R	G	K	I
D	O	G	P	X	D	W	S
M	N	T	K	Z	H	X	V

B. 21 CS Critical Thinking, Life Skills | HQ Coexisting with Nature

Scatter some seeds and some crumbs of chapati in an open area and watch birds come. Observe the birds closely and describe any two different types of birds that you see.

C. 21 CS Critical Thinking, Communication | CC Integration with English

What did the deer tell the lion? Write your answer in the speech bubble.

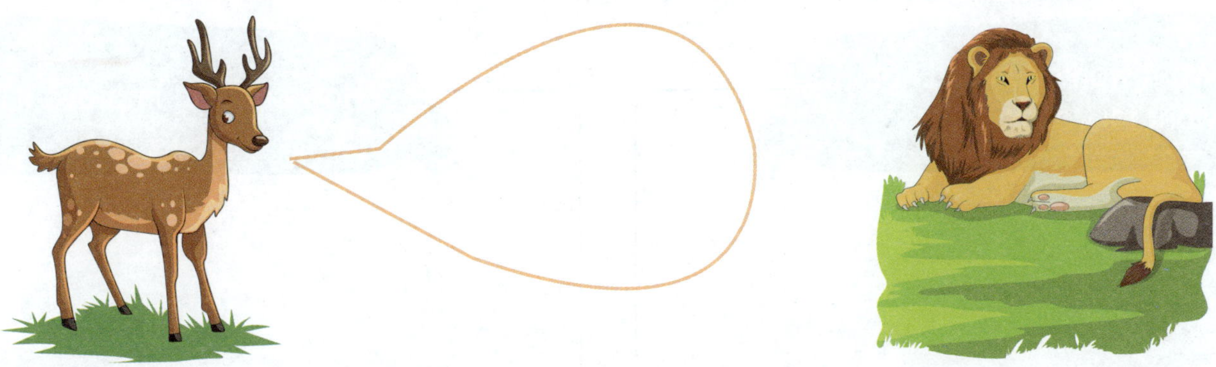

Worksheet 3

STEAM CHALLENGE

Use the following shapes to create your own animals. After you have made your animals, make a model of a jungle. Remember the animals need jungles to live. So, we should not cut trees or else they will be homeless.

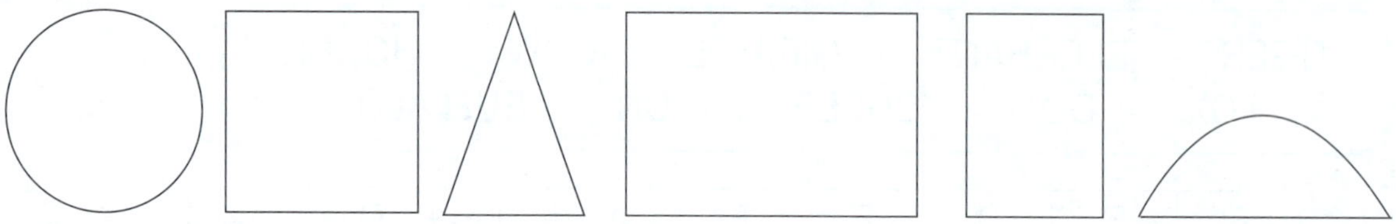

Use your creativity and make a small jungle for your animals.

What is the challenge?

What supplies do you need?

1

2

What worked or did not work for you?

How can you improve it?

9 Parts of Our Body

Prior Knowledge

In the previous classes, I have learnt that

- We know the names of different parts of our body.
- We can do a lot of things with the different parts of our body.
- It is important to keep ourselves clean.

Learning Objectives

In this chapter, I will learn about:

- Parts of our body and their functions
- Sense organs
- Ways to keep ourselves clean and healthy
- Importance of exercise and rest

Let's Get Going

Which parts of your body do you use to do the following activities?

PARTS OF OUR BODY AND THEIR FUNCTIONS

Let us learn the names of the different parts of our body.

Our body has different parts. Each part has a different name and function. For example, we bite with our teeth, dance with our legs, kick a football with our foot and pick a bottle with our hands.

All parts of our body work together to keep us alive and healthy.

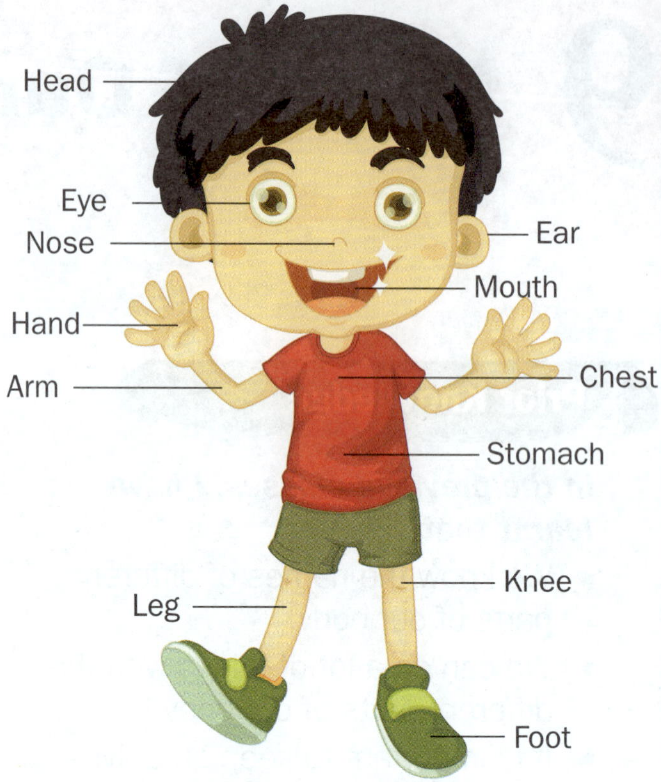

Parts of our body

SENSE ORGANS

Sense organs help us to know what is going on around us. We have five sense organs: eyes, nose, ears, tongue and skin.

Eyes help us to see.

Ears help us to hear.

Tongue helps us to taste.

Nose helps us to smell.

Skin helps us to feel.

Real World

- Our thumb is an important part of our hand. Without a thumb, we would not be able to write, hold anything or eat with our fingers.
- It is our brain that controls what we see, smell, hear, taste and feel.

Knowledge Check

Name the following.

1. Two things that you can see ________________, ________________
2. Two things that you can smell ________________, ________________
3. Two things that you can hear ________________, ________________
4. Two things that you can taste ________________, ________________
5. Two things that you can feel ________________, ________________

WAYS TO KEEP OURSELVES CLEAN AND HEALTHY

To stay healthy, we must eat healthy and drink plenty of water. We must also keep ourselves clean. We have dirt and germs all around us. Sometimes, we can see them and sometimes we cannot see them. They can make us sick. So, we must follow clean habits to avoid falling sick.

Here are some of the ways to keep ourselves clean.

We must practise good toilet habits.

We must brush our teeth two times a day.

We must bathe every day.

We must comb our hair and get our nails clipped regularly.

We must wear clean clothes.

We must wash our hands before and after meals.

Remember that if we do not keep ourselves clean, we will be attacked by germs. Germs can make us fall sick. Thus, it is important for us to follow all these habits to keep ourselves clean.

Real World

We should keep ourselves clean and safe from germs that cause sickness such as COVID-19. We should keep washing our hands regularly or use a sanitizer. We should wear a mask while going out. We should also avoid going to crowded places.

IMPORTANCE OF EXERCISE AND REST

To keep our body healthy, it is important to exercise regularly and take proper rest. It is important that we get at least eight hours of sleep every day. We must go to bed early and wake up early. We must also have fun in our free time.

Stretching

Running

Yoga

Talk About

Name the outdoor games you like to play.

Real World

Walking is a good exercise for people of all ages and it keeps us fit.

Concept Map

Different Parts of Our Body
- Head
- Eyes
- Ears
- Nose
- Mouth
- Hands
- Arms
- Chest
- Stomach
- Legs
- Knees
- Feet

Sense Organs
- Eyes
- Ears
- Nose
- Tongue
- Skin

Looking After Our Body
- Eat healthy
- Exercise regularly
- Keep ourselves clean
- Drink plenty of water
- Get proper amount of sleep

Summary

a. In this chapter, I have learnt that

- Our body has different parts.
- Sense organs help us to feel the world around us.
- To stay healthy, we must keep ourselves clean.
- To keep our body healthy, it is important to exercise regularly and take proper rest.

b. I can do the following:

- Name the different parts of our body
- Use my sense organs to tell what is around us
- Look after myself and stay fit

Practice ZONE

A. Fill in the blanks using the words given in the box.

nose	eyes	hands	ears	teeth

1. I see with my ____________________ .
2. I smell with my ____________________ .
3. I hear with my ____________________ .
4. I bite with my ____________________ .
5. I write with my ____________________ .

B. Match the following.

1. teeth	a. nail cutter
2. body	b. toothpaste
3. nails	c. washing machine
4. clothes	d. towel

C. Give reasons for each of these.

1. The most important sense organ is the eye.

   ____

2. Sleep is as important as food for our body.

   ____

D. Answer these questions.

1. Name the body part that helps us to kick a football.

   ____

2. Name the sense organ that helps you to taste soup.

   ____

3. Which sense organ would you use to see if it is raining outside?

   ____

4. Why should we keep ourselves clean?

____

5. Name two types of exercises.

____

E. Picture Talk

Look at the pictures and name the healthy routine habits followed by Nungsang.

__________ __________ __________

F. Out of the box!

Our elders advise us not to have too many sweets or candies. Do you know why?

____

____

Skills Enrichment ZONE

A. 21 CS Critical Thinking, Life Skills | AI | HQ Knowing My Needs

13 CLIMATE ACTION

What do you do with the wrappers of the things you use? Do you throw those away properly? Collect wrappers of all the things that you use daily such as soap, toothbrush and toothpaste to keep yourself clean. Paste them in your scrapbook.

B. 21 CS Collaboration, Life Skills | EL | CC Integration with Mathematics | HQ How Similar are We

Make a group of five. Draw outlines of your hands on a plain sheet of paper using a pencil or a crayon. Now, compare the sizes of your hands.

10 Keeping Safe

Prior Knowledge

In the previous classes, I have learnt that

- We should be careful at all times to avoid accidents.
- Remembering safety rules keep us safe.

Learning Objectives

In this chapter, I will learn about:

Safety rules

- at home
- on the road
- at school
- in the playground
- in the bus

Let's Get Going

Look at the pictures and talk about why they are not safe.

Safety means keeping oneself away from danger. We can be safe only if we are careful.

SAFETY RULES

We follow certain rules to keep ourselves safe and avoid accidents. These rules are called **safety rules**.

We should follow safety rules whether we are at home or outside. Let us learn about these rules that we should follow.

Safety rules at home

Do not play with scissors.

- Do not play with sharp objects such as knives, scissors, needles or pins. They might hurt you.
- Be careful in the toilet. Do not wet the toilet floor as it might get slippery and you might fall.
- Do not play with electric wires or plug points. They might give you a shock.
- Do not play with matchsticks or go very close to the stove and other hot things as these might start a fire or give you burns.
- Put your toys back in place after playing. Someone might step on them and get hurt.

Do not play with electric wires and plug points.

Do not leave your toys all over the place.

Safety rules on the road

- Always walk on the **footpath**.
- Do not play or walk in the middle of the road.
- Use the **zebra crossing** to cross the road.
- Follow the **traffic lights.** Red light says **stop**, yellow light says **get ready** and green light says **go**.
- Before crossing the road, always look to the right, then to the left and then to the right again. Cross only when the road is clear.
- Follow **pedestrian lights**, if any, to cross the road. Cross only when the pedestrian light is green and wait when it is red.

Safety on the road

My Dictionary

- **zebra crossing:** an area of road marked with black and white stripes where you can cross the road safely
- **pedestrian:** a person walking or moving on foot

Real World

When there is no footpath, you must walk on the left side of the road so that you can see the traffic coming from the front.

Knowledge Check

Put a tick for the correct sentence and a cross for the wrong one.

1. We must follow safety rules only when we are outside the house. ☐
2. When the pedestrian light is red, we must cross the road. ☐
3. Always cross the road at zebra crossing. ☐

Safety rules at school

- Do not run around in the classroom or in the **corridors** as you might hurt yourself.
- Do not play with sharp objects such as scissors, sharpeners and pointed pencils.
- Always walk in a queue, and do not push each other.
- Do not run down the stairs.

Your Task

Does your school have a first-aid box? What things are kept inside a first-aid box?

Do not run in the classroom.

Always walk in a queue.

My Dictionary

corridor: a long passage in a building

Safety rules in the playground

- Do not play rough games.
- Do not fight with your friends.
- Do not stand before a moving swing as it might hit you.
- Always wait for your turn while playing on a swing or a slide.

Do not stand before a moving swing.

Safety rules in the bus

- Sit on your seat and do not stand in a moving bus.
- Never put your head or arm out of the window.
- Stand in a queue while getting in or getting off from a bus.
- Do not shout in a moving bus as it disturbs the driver.

Do not put your arm out of the window.

Concept Map

Safety Rules

- **At home**
  - Do not play with sharp objects.
  - Be careful in the toilet.
  - Do not play with electric wires.
  - Put toys back after playing.
  - Do not play with matchsticks or go near stoves.
- **On the road**
  - Walk on the footpath.
  - Use zebra crossing to cross the road.
  - Follow traffic lights.
  - Cross the road when it is clear of traffic.
  - Follow pedestrian lights.
- **At school**
  - No playing around in the classroom or corridors.
  - Do not play with sharp objects such as scissors, pencils, sharpeners.
  - Always walk in a queue.
  - Do not run down the stairs.
- **In the playground**
  - Do not play rough games.
  - Do not fight with friends.
  - Do not stand before a moving swing.
  - Wait for your turn to play.
- **In the bus**
  - Do not stand in a moving bus.
  - Do not put your head or arm out of the window.
  - Stand in a queue to get in or get off from a bus.
  - Do not shout in a moving bus.

Summary

a. In this chapter, I have learnt that

- We should follow safety rules to keep ourselves safe and avoid accidents.
- We should follow safety rules when we are at home, on the road, at school, in the playground and in the bus.

b. I can do the following:

- Remember that safety rules keep us safe and avoid accidents

Practice ZONE

A. Fill in the blanks using the words given in the box.

rough	footpath	queue	electric	green

1. We should not play with ____________ wires.
2. We should walk on the ____________ .
3. We should cross the road when the pedestrian light is ____________ .
4. Do not play a ____________ game.
5. Stand in a ____________ while getting in or getting off from a bus.

B. Write T for true or F for false.

1. We should not play with electric wires or plug points. ☐
2. We should play or walk in the middle of the road. ☐
3. It is not important to use zebra crossing while crossing the road. ☐
4. We should not put our head or arm out of the window of a bus. ☐

C. Give reasons for each of these.

1. The path to cross the road is called zebra crossing.

____

2. We should not play behind a parked car.

____

D. Answer these questions.

1. Name three sharp things that might hurt you.

____

2. Why should we put our toys back in place after playing?

____

3. Where should we cross the road?

____

4. Why should we not shout in a moving bus?

____

E. Picture Talk

Colour the traffic light. What does each colour of the traffic light tell us?

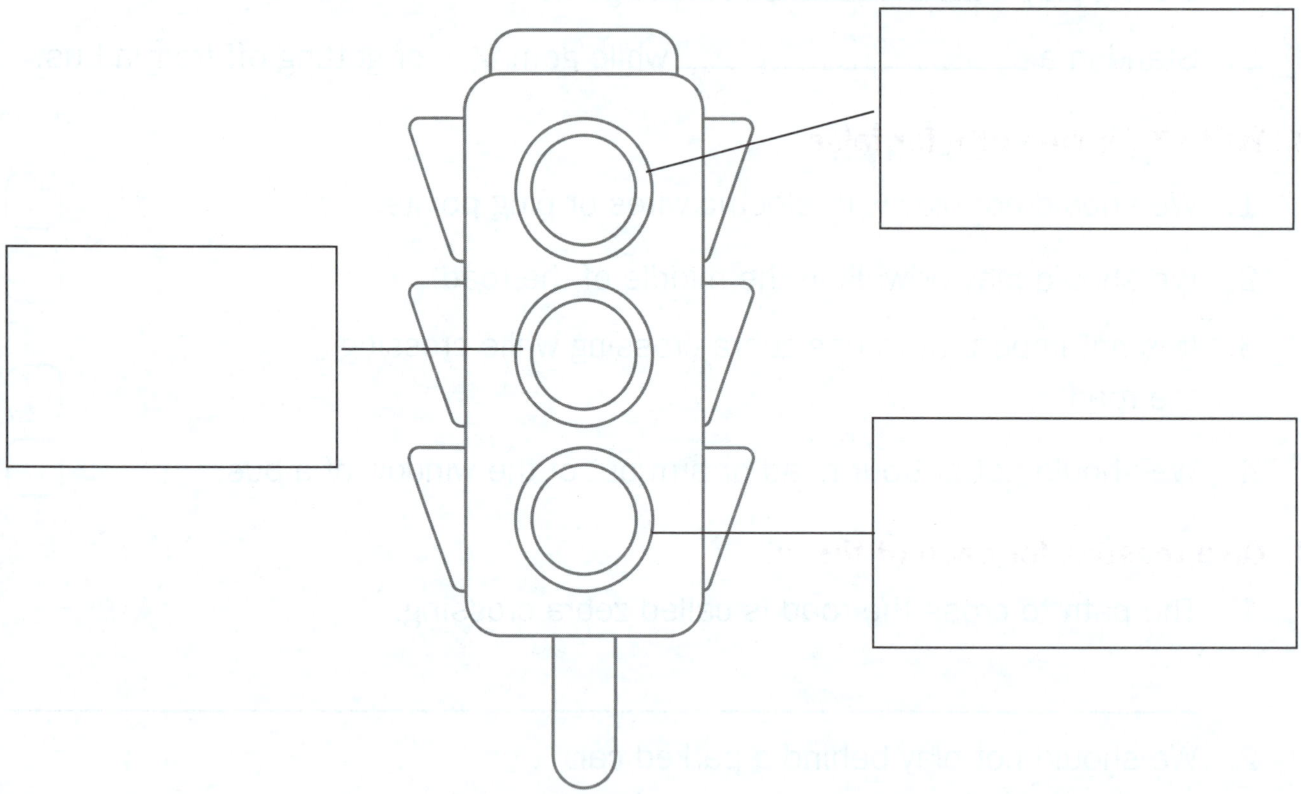

F. Out of the box!

The teacher asks the children to play in the playground and not in the classroom. Why?

____

____

Skills Enrichment ZONE

A. 21 CS Critical Thinking, Life Skills AI HQ Knowing My Needs

Collect and paste pictures of any five things in your scrapbook that you feel can be unsafe at home. Name them and write why these can be harmful to us.

B. 21 CS Critical Thinking, Life Skills HQ Cooperation and Collaborative Living

11 SUSTAINABLE CITIES AND COMMUNITIES

Look at the picture and tick the children who are following safety rules and cross the ones who are not following safety rules.

Worksheet 4

STEAM CHALLENGE

Many students get hurt while playing in the playground. It is always good to keep a few first-aid things in your classroom.

What about making a first-aid box?

Find about the first-aid things and make a first-aid box for your classroom.

What is the challenge?

What supplies do you need?

IDEA 1

IDEA 2

What worked or did not work for you?

How can you improve it?

11 Housing, Clothing and Food

Prior Knowledge

In the previous classes, I have learnt that

- We live in a house.
- We wear clothes to cover our bodies and keep ourselves warm.
- We need food to live.

Learning Objectives

In this chapter, I will learn about:

- Why do we need a house?
- What is a house made up of?
- Why do we need clothes?
- Types of clothes
- Why do we need food?
- Food from plants and animals
- Healthy and junk food

Let's Get Going

Join the dots to find a picture of a house. Now, colour the house to make it look beautiful.

WHY DO WE NEED A HOUSE?

We need a house to live in. A house protects us from cold, rain, wind and heat. It also keeps us safe from thieves and animals. We stay there with our family.

WHAT IS A HOUSE MADE UP OF?

Different houses are made up of different materials. Some houses are made up of bricks, cement, steel, wood and glass. Such houses are strong houses. Some people make their own houses such as huts with mud and dry leaves. Such houses are not strong.

Talk About

- How many people live in the same house with you?
- Where do you play in the evening?

A bungalow is a strong house.

A hut is made of mud, grass and dry leaves.

Different Rooms of a House

A strong house may have many rooms.

A kitchen is where we cook.

A bedroom is where we sleep.

A study room is where we study.

A drawing room is where we spend time with family and friends.

A bathroom is where we wash, bathe and clean ourselves.

A dining room is where we have meals together.

WHY DO WE NEED CLOTHES?

We wear clothes to cover our bodies. Clothes also protect us from heat, rain and cold. We also wear clothes to look good.

Real World

- We get cotton from plants.
- We get wool from sheep.
- We get silk from silkworms.

Types of Clothes

We wear different clothes on different days. For example, on cold days, we should not wear shorts and T-shirts when we go out.

When it is very hot, we wear light **cotton clothes** to keep our body cool.

Hot day

Rainy day

Cold day

On a rainy day, we wear **raincoats** and **gumboots** to protect us from rain. We also carry an **umbrella** to protect ourselves from rain.

We wear **woollen clothes** on cold days to keep our bodies warm.

Talk About

What do children wear when they go to school? Discuss about the special clothes of different people when they go to work.

Remember

Wear clean, well-ironed and comfortable clothes that make you look and feel good.

Knowledge Check

Name the following.

1. I am a house made of mud. ____________
2. I wear these clothes on a hot day. ____________
3. I am a house made of bricks. ____________

WHY DO WE NEED FOOD?

All living things need food to live. Food gives us the energy we need to work and play. We need food to grow and stay healthy.

FOOD WE EAT

We get food from both plants and animals. We get fruits, vegetables, leaves and seeds from plants. We get milk, eggs and meat from animals.

Apple (fruit)

Cabbage (vegetable)

Spinach (leaves)

Pulses (seeds)

Meat

Eggs

HEALTHY AND JUNK FOOD

We should eat healthy food as it keeps us healthy and makes us strong. Some healthy food items are fruits, milk, vegetables, dal and sandwiches.

We should always eat fresh and clean food. We should also drink plenty of water. We should drink at least eight glasses of water in a day.

Junk food items are the food items that are not healthy and make us fat and weak. Sweets, chips, pizzas and fizzy drinks are junk food. We should try to avoid them.

Talk About

Who are vegans?

Real World

You should never skip your breakfast as it is the most important meal of the day. A good breakfast gives you all the energy you need and makes you ready for the day.

MEALS OF THE DAY

We have three main meals in a day. They are **breakfast**, **lunch** and **dinner**. We should have our meals on time.

Breakfast

Lunch

Dinner

Concept Map

Basic Needs

- **House**
  - We live in a house.
  - A house protects us from cold, heat, rain and wind.
  - It keeps us safe from thieves and animals.
  - Strong houses are made of cement, bricks, steel, wood and glass. Huts are made of mud and dry leaves.
- **Clothes**
  - We wear cotton clothes on a hot day.
  - We wear woollen clothes on a cold day.
  - On a rainy day, we wear raincoats and gumboots and carry umbrellas.
- **Food**
  - From plants
    - Fruits, vegetables, leaves and seeds
  - From animals
    - Milk, eggs and meat

Summary

a. In this chapter, I have learnt that

- We need a house to live in. A house protects us from cold, rain, wind and heat.
- We wear clothes to cover our bodies. Clothes also protect us from heat, rain and cold.
- All living things need food to live.
- Food gives us the energy we need to work and play. We need food to grow and stay healthy.
- We should eat healthy food and avoid junk food.

b. I can do the following:

- Help keep my house clean
- Wear clothes according to the weather
- Eat healthy and avoid junk food
- Eat food at the right meal time

Practice ZONE

A. Write T for true or F for false.

1. A strong house is made of mud. ☐
2. All houses have a garden. ☐
3. We wear a raincoat on a rainy day. ☐
4. We get all our food from plants. ☐
5. We should eat vegetables as they keep us healthy. ☐

B. Fill in the blanks using the words given in the box.

seeds	energy	thieves	three	cotton

1. A house protects us from ________________ .
2. Light ________________ clothes keep our body cool.
3. Food gives us ________________ to work and play.
4. We get ________________ from plants.
5. We have ________________ main meals a day.

C. Give reasons for each of these.

1. Mary has a house with a lot of windows.

   ____

2. Anirban is very choosy about his food and always leaves food on the plate. His mother always advises him to eat all his food.

   ____

D. Answer these questions.

1. What are strong houses made of?

____

2. What kind of clothes should we wear when it is very hot?

____

3. Why do we need food?

____

4. Name two food items that we get from animals.

____

5. Why should we avoid junk food?

____

E. Picture Talk

Match the following.

1. Rainy day
2. Cold day
3. Hot day

a. 

b. 

c. 

F. Out of the box!

Lakshmi loves to eat diced fruits (fruit chaat) and often buys it from the roadside shops. Do you think she is doing the right thing? What do you think may happen to her?

____

____

Skills Enrichment ZONE

A. 21 CS Creativity and Innovation, Collaboration EL

Make your own dessert!

a. Take some salted biscuits.

b. Take strawberry jam and cream cheese (or hung curd) and mix them.

c. With the help of an elder, spoon them over the biscuits in twirls.

d. You may use other types of jams too.

B. 21 CS Communication, Life Skills HQ Cooperation and Collaborative Living

2 ZERO HUNGER

Play this game with your friends. One of your friend says, 'I am going to make soup today and I am going to add some (name of an ingredient such as salt, pepper or vegetables)'. The second friend repeats what the first friend said and adds one more item. The game continues with each person adding another item to the list. If someone forgets, the game starts over again.

Did you like the game? Did it give you any idea about food and its importance?

Do you know that 1 out of every 9 people on the Earth go to bed hungry every night? Imagine how they would feel!

Worksheet 5

STEAM CHALLENGE

Your teacher has asked you to design a small house using materials such as twigs, fallen leaves and small stones.

Go on a nature walk to collect material and make your own house.

What is the challenge?

What supplies do you need?

IDEA 1

IDEA 2

What worked or did not work for you?

How can you improve it?

12 Transport

Prior Knowledge

In the previous classes, I have learnt that

- We need transport to go from one place to another.
- I know the names of different means of transport.

Learning Objectives

In this chapter, I will learn about:

Different means of transport

- land transport
- water transport
- air transport

Let's Get Going

Transport is something that is used to move people or goods from one place to another. Fill in the missing letters to spell the different means of transport.

__U__

A__R__P__A__ __

S__I__B__A__

DIFFERENT MEANS OF TRANSPORT

We use different means of transport to go from one place to another. We also use transport to carry goods.

There are three means of transport.

- Land transport
- Water transport
- Air transport

Land Transport

> **My Dictionary**
>
> **vehicle:** something that carries people or goods from one place to another

Different **vehicles** that move on land are the means of **land transport**. Land transport can be of two types:

- Road transport
- Rail transport

Vehicles such as trucks, buses, cars, motorcycles, bicycles, rickshaws and autorickshaws move on road and are called the means of **road transport**. Some of them move fast such as cars and buses, while some of them move slow such as bullock carts and bicycles.

Truck

Motorcycle

Bicycle

Rickshaw

Autorickshaw

Trains move on railway tracks or rails. They are the means of **rail transport**.

Trains move fast and can carry many passengers and goods at the same time over a long distance. Metro and trams also move on tracks.

Talk About

Smoke from vehicles make the air dirty. Can you name two means of transport that do not give out smoke and do not make the air dirty?

Train

Metro

Means of land transport can also be grouped on the basis of the number of wheels they have.

Two-wheels	Three-wheels	Four-wheels	More than four-wheels
Bicycle	Tricycle	Car	Train
Motorcycle	Rickshaw	Van	Truck
Scooter	Autorickshaw	Jeep	Metro

Knowledge Check

Write T for True or F for False.

1. Vehicles that move on the road are the means of land transport. ☐
2. Bicycles are the means of transport that move very fast. ☐
3. A truck is a means of rail transport. ☐
4. A metro moves on tracks. ☐

Water Transport

The means of transport that move on water are called **water transport**. They take us across rivers, lakes and oceans. Ships can carry a lot of people and goods in them.

Ship

Boat

Yacht

Real World

A submarine is a warship that can travel under water. It may travel above and below the surface of the sea.

Air Transport

The means of transport that move in the air are called **air transport**. They are the fastest means of transport and move at a very high speed. An aeroplane can carry a lot of people and goods over a long distance in a short time.

Talk About

Do you think an aeroplane has wheels? If yes, what are they used for?

Aeroplane

Helicopter

Concept Map

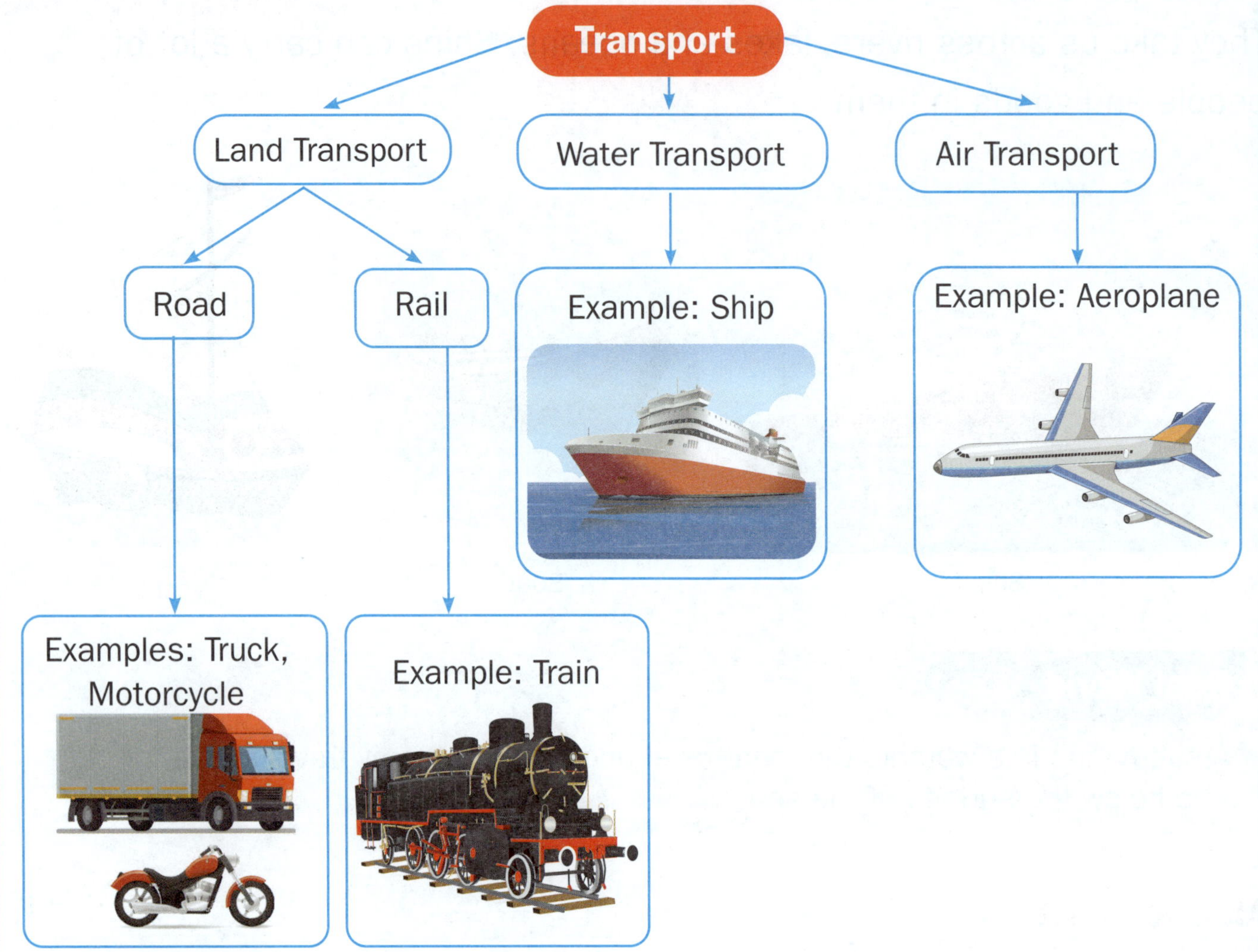

Summary

a. In this chapter, I have learnt that

- We use different means of transport to go from one place to another and to carry goods.
- There are three means of transport: land transport, air transport and water transport.
- Land transport can be of two types: road transport and rail transport.

b. I can do the following:

- Use different means of transport to go to places
- Name different means of land, water and air transport

Practice ZONE

A. Name the following.

1. Two means of transport that move on rails ________, ________
2. Two means of transport that move in water ________, ________
3. Two three-wheeled vehicles ________, ________
4. Two of the fastest means of transport ________, ________

B. Match the following.

1. Air	a. Van
2. Road	b. Yacht
3. Rail	c. Aeroplane
4. Water	d. Metro

C. Give reasons for each of these.

1. To go to a nearby market, we should walk or go on a bicycle.

____

2. Some trucks have more than four wheels.

____

D. Answer these questions in brief.

1. Why do we need transport?

____

2. Name two means of transport that move on land.

____

3. Name two vehicles that have more than four wheels.

____

4. Why are trains a useful means of transport?

____

E. Picture Talk

Put the following means of transport from the fastest to the slowest in order. Number them from 1 to 5 (5 being the fastest).

F. Out of the box!

Can you use a bullock cart to go to another country?

____

____

Skills Enrichment ZONE

A. 21 CS Communication, Creativity and Innovation | AI | HQ Harmony in the Self

9 INDUSTRY, INNOVATION AND INFRASTRUCTURE

Draw your dream car that you want to own when you grow up. Then, talk about how it will be different from the cars you see on the roads now.

B. 21 CS Life Skills | HQ Coexisting with Nature

13 CLIMATE ACTION

3 GOOD HEALTH AND WELL-BEING

Try to walk or ride a bicycle to go to nearby places. This would not only help in reducing smoke from cars but also act as a good form of exercise. What other things can you do to reduce smoke from cars?

Worksheet 6

STEAM CHALLENGE

You like to travel in aeroplane and want to become a pilot when you grow up. You are going to fly a unique aeroplane.

Use your imagination and creativity to make a model of the aeroplane that you are going to fly.

What is the challenge?

What supplies do you need?

1

2

What worked or did not work for you?

How can you improve it?

13 Air, Water and Weather

Prior Knowledge

In the previous classes, I have learnt that

- We can feel air but we cannot see it.
- We need air and water to live.
- Some days are hot, some days are cold and some days are rainy.

Learning Objectives

In this chapter, I will learn about:

- Air is everywhere
- Uses of air
- Sources of water
- Uses of water
- Saving water
- Weather
- Seasons

Let's Get Going

A. When we blow into a balloon, it gets filled with ___________.

B. When you enter a room and switch on the fan, you feel the ___________ moving.

C. Look outside and describe the weather.

1. Is it (warm/cold)?
2. Is it (sunny/cloudy)?
3. Is it raining outside? (yes/no)
4. Is the sun shining (bright/not so bright)?
5. Is it a windy day? (yes/no)

AIR IS EVERYWHERE

Air is everywhere. We can feel air when it moves but cannot see it. Moving air is called **wind**.

Air takes up space

Air filled inside a balloon or a football gives it a shape. This shows that air takes up space.

Blown-up balloon

Air filled in football

Air has weight

A blown-up balloon is heavier than a flat one. This shows that air has weight.

Flat balloon

USES OF AIR

- All living things need air to breathe.
- Air helps to move things such as windmills and sailboats.
- Air helps to dry wet clothes.
- Air helps things such as aeroplanes and kites to fly.
- Air is used to fill up footballs, tyres of cars and bicycles, and balloons.
- Air helps in burning.

Girl breathing

Drying clothes

Real World

We make the air dirty by burning crackers, leaves and tyres. We also make the air unclean with the smoke that comes out of chimneys or cars.

Let's Try

Ask your mother to light a candle. Now place the candle on a plate and cover it with a glass.

Write what you see after a few minutes?

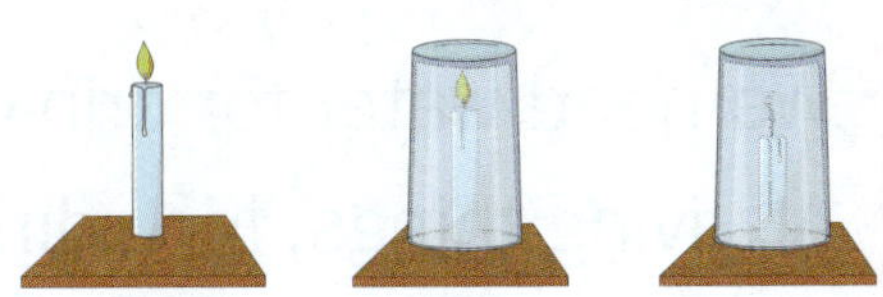

____

This happens because air helps in burning.

Knowledge Check

Write T for true or F for false.

1. We cannot feel air.
2. Air has weight.
3. Air helps sailboat to fly.
4. Air helps to dry wet clothes.

SOURCES OF WATER

River

Well

All living things need water to live.

Rain is the main source of water. Water also comes from rivers, ponds, lakes, seas and oceans. Some rainwater goes into the ground. We dig wells or use hand pumps to pump out water from under the ground.

At home, we store water in bottles, buckets, drums and clay pots. Large amount of water is stored in tanks and **dams**.

Dam

Bottle

My Dictionary

dam: a wall built across a river to hold back water

Talk About

What do you use at home to make water fit for drinking?

USES OF WATER

- We need water for drinking, cooking, bathing and washing.
- All living things, including plants, need water to live.
- We need water to put out fire.
- We use water as a means of transport to move from one place to another.

Your Task

Take two potted plants and put them on your window sill. Water one plant daily and do not water the other one. What do you see after a few days? What does it tell you?

How to save water?

- Close the tap properly after use.
- Keep the tap closed while brushing your teeth.
- Use a bucket and a mug while having a bath.

Save water while brushing your teeth.

WEATHER

Weather changes from day to day. Some days are very hot, while some days are cold. Sometimes it rains a lot, while sometimes it is dry. The weather is connected to the sun, wind and the clouds.

SEASONS

When the weather remains more or less the same for a few months, we call it a **season**. The five main seasons of India are spring, summer, monsoon (rainy), autumn and winter.

Spring season

In the spring season, new leaves appear on trees. Birds chirp around and make nests to lay eggs. Flowers bloom. The days are **pleasant** and everyone likes to go for picnics.

Spring season

My Dictionary

pleasant: neither hot nor cold

Summer season

Summer season

Summer is the hottest season of the year. The sun shines brightly and the days are hot. We wear light cotton clothes. In the summer season, we like to stay indoors and be near the fan or an air conditioner.

Monsoon season

Monsoon season

In India, it rains a lot during the monsoon season. The farmers wait for the rains as it helps crops to grow. We carry an umbrella or wear a raincoat and gumboots to school when it rains.

Autumn season

Autumn season

Autumn is the season which comes before winter. The days start getting cooler. In cold places, the leaves of some trees turn orange, brown or yellow and fall off.

Winter season

Winter season

Winter is the coldest season of the year. The days and nights are cold. In winter, we like to play in the sunshine. People wear woollen clothes.

Real World

During winter, days are short and nights are long. In summer, days are long and nights are short.

Talk About

- Write two things that you like to eat or drink in the summer season.
- What change do you feel in the autumn season?

Concept Map

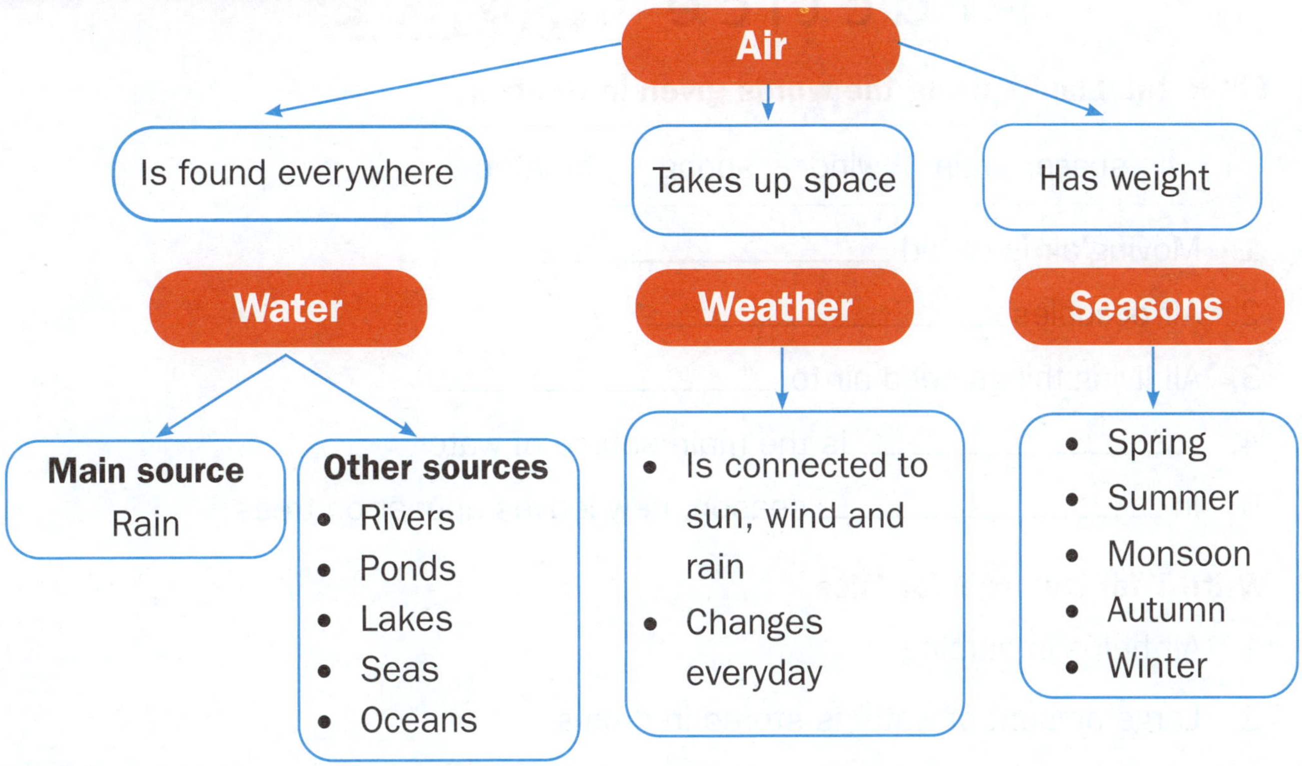

Summary

a. In this chapter, I have learnt that

- We can feel air but cannot see it.
- Rain is the main source of water.
- Water is needed for drinking, cooking, bathing and washing.
- Weather changes from day to day.
- Weather is connected to the sun, wind and clouds.
- When the weather remains more or less the same for a few months, we call it a season.
- There are five seasons. Winter is the coldest season and summer is the hottest season.

b. I can do the following:

- Feel the air
- Save water
- Describe the weather outside
- Name the five seasons
- Dress according to the seasons

Practice ZONE

A. Fill in the blanks using the words given in the box.

space	rain	wind	spring	breathe

1. Moving air is called ____________________.
2. Air occupies ____________________.
3. All living things need air to ____________________.
4. ____________________ is the main source of water.
5. In ____________________ season, new leaves appear on trees.

B. Write T for true or F for false.

1. Air helps in burning. ☐
2. Large amount of water is stored in drums. ☐
3. Autumn comes before summer. ☐
4. Farmers wait for the rains. ☐
5. The days are pleasant in spring season. ☐

C. Give reasons for each of these.

1. We shall not survive if there is no air on Earth.

   ____

2. We should not waste water.

   ____

D. Answer these questions.

1. How can you show that air occupies space?

   ____

2. Name some sources of water.

   ____

3. What is weather connected to?

___

4. What is a season?

___

5. Name the five seasons.

___

E. Picture Talk

Look at the pictures and identify the weather.

___ ___ ___

F. Out of the box!

1. How can we reuse water from the kitchen?

___

2. Your class is going out for a picnic on 10th August. The class teacher asks all the children to pack a raincoat. Why?

___

Skills Enrichment ZONE

A. 21 CS Creativity and Innovation, Life Skills AI EL

Make your own paper plane.

1. Take a rectangular piece of paper. Fold it along the dotted line to meet the centre line.
2. Fold it along the dotted line as shown in the picture.
3. Fold it along the dotted line to meet the centre line.
4. Fold it along the line as shown in the picture.
5. Fold it backward along the line as shown in the picture.
6. Fold it along the dotted line. Your paper plane is ready.

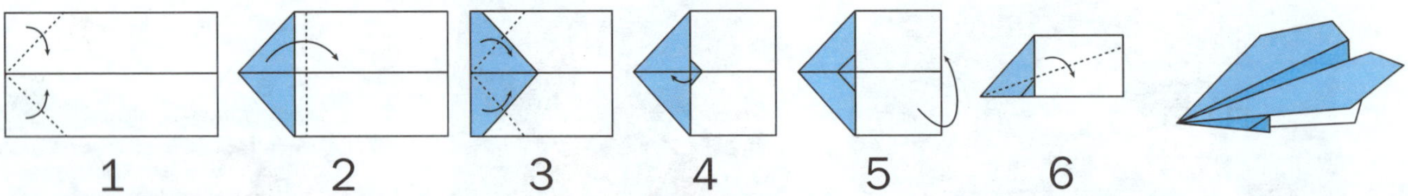

B. 21 CS Critical Thinking, Life Skills CC Integration with Social Studies HQ Coexisting with Nature

6 CLEAN WATER AND SANITATION 13 CLIMATE ACTION

Monsoon brings us rain. However, nowadays it does not rain that much due to climate change. There is shortage of water and farmers are unable to grow crops properly. Also, many people on Earth do not have enough clean water to drink.

Now, think whether you have ever wasted water. Knowing there is shortage of water on Earth, what would you do now? Make a poster to share your thoughts.

14 Our Earth and the Sky

Prior Knowledge

In the previous classes, I have learnt that

- We live on Earth.
- Earth is made up of land and water.
- We see the sun, moon, clouds, stars and rainbow in the sky.

Learning Objectives

In this chapter, I will learn about:

- Earth
- Hills, mountains and plains
- Water bodies on Earth
- Taking care of the Earth
- Sun, moon, clouds, stars and rainbow

Let's Get Going

A. Look at the picture and name five things that you see.

1. ________________
2. ________________
3. ________________
4. ________________
5. ________________

B. What objects do you see in the sky?

In the day ....

At night ....

EARTH

The planet on which we live is called the **Earth**. It is the only **planet** known to have air and water. That is why it is called a living planet. The surface of our planet is made up of **land** and **water**. There is more water than land on Earth.

My Dictionary

planet: a large round object in space that moves around a star

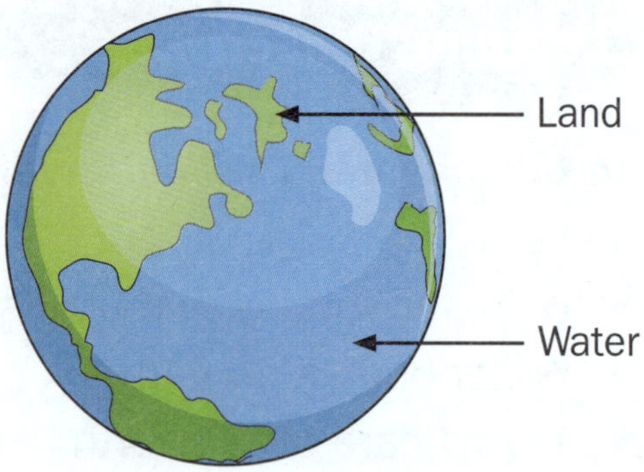

Real World

The Earth is round in shape. A globe is a model of the Earth.

Trees, hills, mountains, oceans, rivers, lakes, ponds, birds, animals and even humans belong to the Earth.

HILLS, MOUNTAINS AND PLAINS

The land part of the Earth is not the same everywhere. Some parts of the land are high and are called **hills**. Very high hills are called **mountains**. They are covered with snow.

Your Task

What is the name of the highest mountain on Earth? Where is it located?

The flat parts of the Earth are called **plains**. Most people live on the plains as it is easy to grow crops there.

Hills

Mountains

Plains

WATER BODIES ON THE EARTH

A **sea** is a large area of water. An **ocean** is larger than a sea.

We also find water in **rivers**, **lakes**, **ponds** and **puddles**.

Ocean

River

Lake

TAKING CARE OF THE EARTH

Our Earth gives us all the things that we need. So, we must take care of it.

We must:

- not waste water
- save electricity
- grow more plants and trees, and not cut them
- stop using things made of plastic

Knowledge Check

Fill in the blanks.

1. The surface of the Earth is made up of ______________ and ______________.
2. Snow can be found on ______________.
3. It is easy to grow crops on the ______________.
4. An ______________ is larger than a sea.
5. We must stop using things made of ______________.

IN THE SKY

What do we see in the sky?

The Sun

We see the sun in the sky in the daytime. The sun is round and hot. It is the brightest thing we see in the day sky.

It gives us heat and light.

Sun gives us heat and light

Plants need sunlight to grow.

A new day begins when the sun rises in the **east**. When the day is over, the sun sets in the **west** and the night begins.

Sunrise

Sunset

Talk About

Nothing can grow or live on this Earth without the sun. Why?

On cloudy days, we cannot see the sun as it is hidden behind the clouds.

The Moon

The moon is seen in the sky at night. It has no light of its own. The light of the sun makes the moon glow. The moon changes its shape every day.

Sometimes we see the full round moon and sometimes we see no moon at all. Sometimes we see only a part of it.

We cannot see the moon in the daytime because of the bright light of the sun. The moon looks big as it is closer to the Earth. It is smaller than the Earth and much smaller than the sun.

Different shapes of the moon

Real World

- There is no air or water on the moon. That is why nothing can live or grow there.
- Neil Armstrong was the first person to walk on the moon.

Let's Try

Observe the shape of the moon every night at a fixed time. Now write the date and draw the shape of the moon in the table given below.

	Day 1	Day 2	Day 3	Day 4	Day 5	Day 6	Day 7
Date							
Shape							

Knowledge Check

Fill in the blanks.

1. ____________ gives us heat and light.
2. The sun rises in the ____________ and sets in the ____________.
3. The moon looks so big because it is ____________ to the Earth.

Clouds

Clouds are white fluffy cotton-like things that float across the sky. Dark clouds give us rain.

White clouds

Dark clouds

Stars

When you look at the sky at night, you will see thousands of twinkling stars. The stars make nice **patterns** in the sky.

Stars are big balls of fire. The stars are very big in size. But they look small as they are very far away from us.

My Dictionary

patterns: designs

Stars in the sky

Real World

- Sun is also a star.
- The stars that look small to us may be bigger than the sun.

Rainbow

Sometimes, we see a rainbow in the sky when the sun shines after rain. The rainbow has seven colours. They are violet, indigo, blue, green, yellow, orange and red (VIBGYOR).

A rainbow

Concept Map

- **Earth**
  - Land
    - Mountain
    - Hills
    - Plains
  - Water
    - Oceans
    - Seas
    - Rivers
    - Lakes
- **Sky**
  - Sun
  - Moon
  - Clouds
  - Stars
  - Rainbow

Summary

a. In this chapter, I have learnt that

- The planet Earth is a living planet because it has both air and water.
- The land part of the Earth is made up of hills, mountains and plains.
- We find water on the Earth in seas, oceans, rivers, lakes, ponds and puddles.
- Sun is round and hot. It gives us heat and light.
- We see the moon and stars at night.
- Stars are big balls of fire. They look small because they are very far away from us.
- We see a rainbow in the sky when the sun shines after rain.

b. I can do the following:

- Name the things that make up the Earth
- Take care of the Earth
- Tell the difference between the morning sky and the night sky
- See the shape of the moon changing every day

Practice ZONE

A. Write T for true or F for false.

1. There is more water than land on Earth. ☐
2. The hills are covered with snow. ☐
3. The sun is a star. ☐
4. The sun sets in the east. ☐
5. We see a rainbow after the rain stops. ☐

B. Complete the sentences.

1. The surface of our planet is made up of ____________________.
2. The Earth is the only planet that has ____________________.
3. The stars look small as ____________________.
4. The colours of the rainbow are ____________________.

C. Give reasons for each of these.

1. The plains are different from the mountains.

   ____

2. We shall not survive if the sun stops shining.

   ____

D. Answer these questions.

1. Why is the Earth called the living planet?

   ____

2. Why do we find many people living on the plains?

   ____

3. Name three water bodies present on the Earth.

   ____

4. Why cannot we see the sun on a cloudy day?

   ____

E. Picture Talk

Colour the land part of the Earth green and the water part blue.

F. Out of the box!

Why should we not cut trees?

____

____

Skills Enrichment ZONE

A. 21 CS Critical Thinking, Collaboration HQ Coexisting with Nature

13 CLIMATE ACTION

Make a team with one of your classmate. Discuss how you can keep the Earth clean and make it smile.

B. 21 CS Creativity and Innovation, Collaboration AI EL CC Integration with Computer Science

Take a black chart paper and a white chart paper to show the night sky and the morning sky. With the help of an elder, search on the Internet and find the pictures of stars, moon, sun, clouds and other things that you may find in the sky. Take printouts of the pictures, cut out their shapes and stick them on the chart paper. Talk about how they are different.

C. 21 CS Critical Thinking, Life Skills CC Integration with English HQ Coexisting with Nature

Complete the following.

1. Unscramble the letters to find a hidden message.

VSAE	EHT	OTEHRM	EHTRA
____________	____________	____________	____________

2. Write one rhyming word for these words.

Star	Sky	Cloud	Moon
____________	____________	____________	____________

Worksheet 7

STEAM CHALLENGE

Arif and Ahana are very interested to know about the objects seen in the sky. They decided to collect information about the objects seen in the sky in the day time and at night.

Can you help them to collect the necessary information and make a simple model of the day sky and the night sky?

What is the challenge?

What supplies do you need?

IDEA 1

IDEA 2

What worked or did not work for you?

How can you improve it?

Review Corner

Review 1 (Chapters 1–5) **(Maximum Marks = 25)**

A. Fill in the blanks. (1 × 5 = 5)

1. My mother and father are my ____________________.
2. My father's brother is my ____________________.
3. A ____________________ grows food for us.
4. We must use the ____________________ to throw pencil shavings.
5. ____________________ is the festival of lights.

B. Write T for true or F for false. (1 × 5 = 5)

1. We buy things of our daily use from a supermarket. ☐
2. We go to school only to study. ☐
3. We make *gujiya* on Eid. ☐
4. A small family has more than six members. ☐
5. We keep our money and jewellery in a bank. ☐

C. Match the following. (1 × 4 = 4)

1. Independence Day	a. 26 January
2. Republic Day	b. 2 October
3. Gandhi Jayanti	c. 25 December
4. Christmas	d. 15 August

D. Answer these questions. (2 × 4 = 8)

1. What are national festivals?
2. Who are our neighbours?
3. How does a policeman help us?
4. Write any one rule that you must follow in school.

E. Colour the picture and complete the following sentence. (3 × 1 = 3)

A ________________________ is a place for children to play.

Review 2 (Chapters 6–8) **(Maximum Marks = 25)**

A. Fill in the blanks. (1 × 5 = 5)

1. Trees have hard woody stems called ________________________.
2. An insect has ________________________ legs.
3. ________________________ is a small plant.
4. A squirrel lives on ________________________.
5. A ________________________ is a bird that cannot fly.

B. Give answers in one word. (1 × 5 = 5)

1. A farm animal ________________________
2. An insect with no wings ________________________
3. A seed we eat ________________________

4. Very big plants ____________

5. Animals with feathers and beaks ____________

C. Choose the correct option. **(2 × 2 = 4)**

1. What does the picture show?

   a. Living things grow.

   b. Living things breathe.

   c. Living things need food.

2. Where does the given animal live?

   a. On land

   b. In water

   c. Both on land and in water

D. Answer these questions. **(2 × 4 = 8)**

1. Name the different places where plants grow.
2. What are pet animals?
3. Give two examples of birds that cannot fly.
4. What do plants need to grow?

E. Identify the following parts of the plant and write their functions. **(3 × 1 = 3)**

Review 3 (Chapters 9–10) **(Maximum Marks = 25)**

A. Write T for true or F for false. (1 × 5 = 5)

1. We must clip our nails every day. ☐
2. Germs make us sick. ☐
3. We must cross the road when the pedestrian light is red. ☐
4. We should walk on the footpath. ☐
5. Skin helps us to taste. ☐

B. Fill in the blanks. (1 × 5 = 5)

1. Stand in a ________________ while getting in or getting off a bus.
2. It is important that we get at least ________________ hours of sleep every day.
3. ________________ is a type of exercise.
4. Nose helps us to ________________.
5. Use ________________ to cross the road.

C. Choose the correct option. (2 × 2 = 4)

1. Look at the boxes. Which part of the body shows the wrong function?

a. Eyes b. Skin c. Nose

2. Which of the following shows the correct set of sense organs used while eating a pizza?
    a. Tongue and ears
    b. Nose and tongue
    c. Eyes, nose, tongue and skin

D. Answer these questions. (2 × 4 = 8)

1. What are sense organs?
2. What should we do to keep our body healthy?
3. Why do we follow safety rules?
4. What should we do to keep our mind cheerful?

E. Colour the traffic lights and complete the following sentence. (3 × 1 = 3)

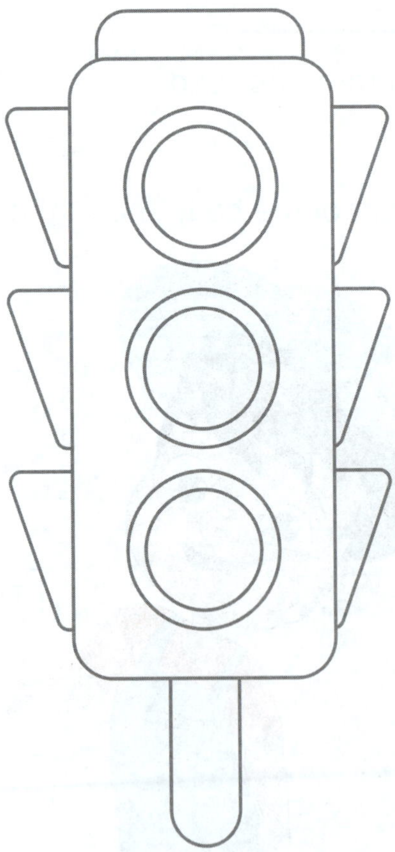

Always ____________ when the traffic light is red, ____________ when it is yellow and ____________ when it is green.

Review 4 (Chapters 11–12) (Maximum Marks = 25)

A. Fill in the blanks. (1 × 5 = 5)

1. ______________ is a strong house made of many floors.
2. We wear ______________ clothes in summer.
3. Food gives us ______________ to work and to play.
4. ______________ moves on tracks.
5. A means of transport that has three wheels is ______________.

B. Name the following. (1 × 5 = 5)

1. A person who wears a uniform to work ______________
2. A plant food that we eat ______________
3. Strong house with one or two floors ______________
4. A house made of mud ______________
5. Means of transport that moves on water ______________

C. Choose the correct option. (2 × 2 = 4)

1. Too much of which food makes you unhealthy?

a.  b.  c. 

2. Which of the following is not a water transport?

a.  b.  c. 

D. Answer these questions. (2 × 4 = 8)

1. Why do we need clothes?
2. What are strong houses made of?
3. What are the three means of transport?
4. What do we get from plants?

E. Colour the picture and complete the following sentence. **(3 × 1 = 3)**

We spend time with our family members and friends in the ____________ room.

Review 5 (Chapters 13–14) **(Maximum Marks = 25)**

A. Fill in the blanks. **(1 × 5 = 5)**

1. We must ____________ the tap properly after use.
2. Moving air is called ____________.
3. ____________ is the main source of water.
4. In India, it rains a lot in the ____________ season.
5. A rainbow has ____________ colours.

B. Match the following. **(1 × 5 = 5)**

1. Very high hills	a. Rain
2. Flat lands	b. Mountains
3. A large area of water	c. Plains
4. Sun	d. Sea
5. Dark clouds	e. Star

C. Choose the correct option. **(2 × 2 = 4)**

1. Which of the following shows air occupies space?

a. 

b. 

c. 

2. Which of the following shows the autumn season?

a. 

b. 

c. 

D. Answer these questions. **(2 × 4 = 8)**

1. How is the weather different from seasons?
2. Why is the Earth called a living planet?
3. Write two ways in which you can take care of the Earth.
4. Name the hottest and the coldest season.

E. Colour the picture and complete the following sentence. **(3 × 1 = 3)**

We wear ________________ clothes in winter season.

National Symbols of India

National Emblem

सत्यमेव जयते

National Flower

Lotus

National Flag

Our national flag has three colours: saffron (at the top), white (in the middle) and green (at the bottom). There is a blue wheel at the centre with twenty-four spokes, known as the Ashoka Chakra.

National Anthem

Jana-gana-mana-adhinayaka jaya he
Bharata-bhagya-vidhata
Punjaba-Sindhu-Gujarata-Maratha
Dravida-Utkala-Banga
Vindhya-Himachala-Yamuna-Ganga
Uchchala-jaladhi-taranga
Tava Subha name jage,
Tava subha asisa mage,
Gahe tava jaya-gatha.
Jana-gana-mangala-dayaka jaya he
Bharata-bhagya-vidhata.
Jaya he, jaya he, jaya he,
Jaya jaya jaya jaya he.

Written by Rabindranath Tagore

National Tree

Banyan Tree

National Fruit

Mango

National Animal

Tiger

National Bird

Peacock

CLASS 1

QUESTION PAPER SET A

SOF NATIONAL SCIENCE OLYMPIAD 2020-21

DO NOT OPEN THIS BOOKLET UNTIL ASKED TO DO SO

Total Questions: 35 | Time: 1 hr.

Guidelines for the Candidate

1. You will get additional ten minutes to fill up information about yourself on the OMR Sheet, before the start of the exam.
2. Write your **Name, School Code, Class, Section, Roll No.** and **Mobile Number** clearly on the **OMR Sheet** and do not forget to sign it. We will share your marks / result and other information related to SOF exams on your mobile number.
3. The Question Paper comprises three sections:

   Logical Reasoning (5 Questions), **Science** (25 Questions) and **Achievers Section** (5 Questions)

   Each question in Achievers Section carries 2 marks, whereas all other questions carry one mark each.
4. All questions are compulsory. There is no negative marking. Use of calculator is not permitted.
5. There is only ONE correct answer. Choose only ONE option for an answer.
6. To mark your choice of answers by darkening the circles on the OMR Sheet, use **HB Pencil** or **Blue / Black ball point pen** only. E.g.

   Q. 16: Raj goes to school on a bicycle. Which of these safety rules he should follow?

   A. He should give signals before taking turns. B. He should keep to the right of the road.

   C. He should cross the road by using zebra crossing. D. All of these

   As the correct answer is option A, you must darken the circle corresponding to option A on the OMR Sheet. 16. ● Ⓑ Ⓒ Ⓓ
7. Rough work should be done in the blank space provided in the booklet.
8. Return the OMR Sheet to the invigilator at the end of the exam.
9. Please fill in your personal details in the space provided on this page before attempting the paper.

SCIENCE OLYMPIAD FOUNDATION

Inspiring Young Minds Through Knowledge Olympiads

Name:..

Section:............ SOF Olympiad Roll No.:.. Contact No.:..

1. Select the odd one out.

A.  B.  C.  D. 

---

2. ________ groups of 3 deer each can be formed from the given deer.

A. 3 B. 6 C. 4 D. 8

---

3. Which of the following options will complete the pattern in the given figure?

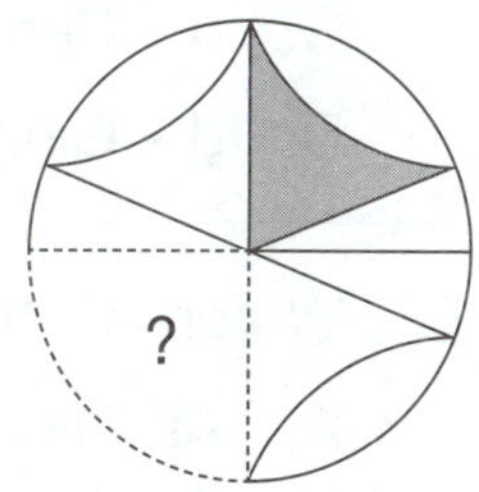

A. 

B. 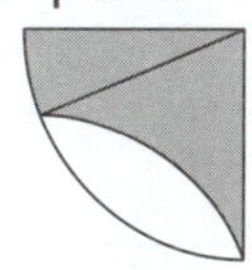

C. 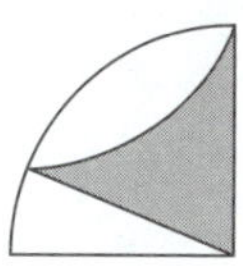

D. 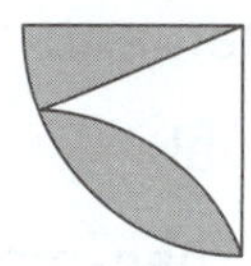

---

4. How many mangoes are there in the figure?

A. 10
B. 12
C. 15
D. 13

---

5. Nimit's birthday falls on 2nd Saturday of November 20XX. On which date is Nimit's birthday?

NOVEMBER 20XX						
Sun	Mon	Tue	Wed	Thu	Fri	Sat
1	2	3	4	5	6	7
8	9	10	11	12	13	14
15	16	17	18	19	20	21
22	23	24	25	26	27	28
29	30					

A. 7th November
B. 8th November
C. 14th November
D. 15th November

SPACE FOR ROUGH WORK

6. Sushant has made the following table about characteristics of living and non-living things, but he made a mistake. Identify the mistake and select the correct option.

	Characteristics	Living things	Non-living things
P.	Breathe	Yes	No
Q.	Feel	Yes	No
R.	Reproduce	No	Yes
S.	Grow	Yes	No

A. P B. Q C. R D. S

---

7. We eat different parts of different plants. Study the given classification chart and select the correct option to fill empty spaces d and e.

A. d - Carrot, e - Broccoli
B. d - Radish, e - Cabbage
C. d - Carrot, e - Onion
D. d - Ginger, e - Cauliflower

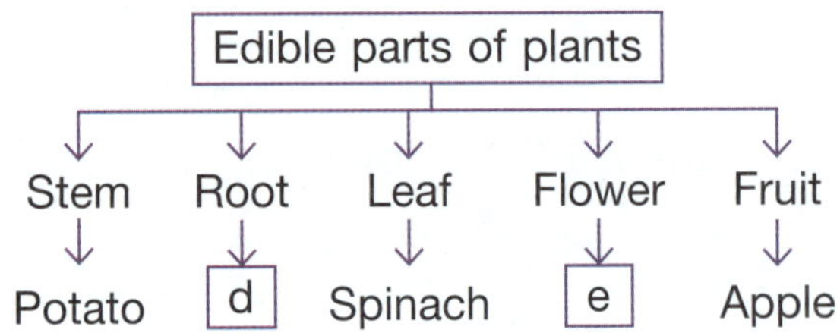

---

8. Which of the following statements is correct?
A. All living things are natural.
B. All non-living things are man-made.
C. All living things can move from one place to another.
D. All non-living things can grow and increase in size.

---

9. Ravi saw a plant in his garden which had beautiful flowers. When he tried to pluck a flower, his finger got pricked. The plant could be _______.
A. Dahlia B. Jasmine C. Rose D. Marigold

---

10. Read the given sentence.

Aditya wore a sweater when he felt cold.

This sentence indicates that living things __________.
A. Grow and die
B. Reproduce
C. Can feel
D. Need air, food and water

SPACE FOR ROUGH WORK

11. Which of the following is both plant and animal eater?

A.  B.  C.  D. 

12. Which of the following flowers is the part of a plant that bears floating leaf?

A.  B.  C.  D. 

13. Select the correct match.

	Animal	**Young one**
A.	Elephant	Cub
B.	Lion	Calf
C.	Dog	Chick
D.	Horse	Foal

14. Siya paired one living thing and one non-living thing together but in doing so she made an incorrect pair.

Select the incorrect pair.

A. Bird - Mountain

B. Fish – Clock

C. Rose plant – Cycle

D. River – Book

15. Which of the following rooms is used for cooking food?

A.  B.  C.  D. 

16. I live in a shed. Who am I?

A.  B.  C.  D. 

SPACE FOR ROUGH WORK

17. All the given animals build a home to live in except ________.

A. Spider B. Bee C. Monkey D. Bird

18. Read the given passage.

You can get an electric __p__ if you touch plug points with wet hands. Do not play with knives and blades, you can get a __q__.

Select the correct option to complete the passage.

	p	q
A.	Shock	Cut
B.	Burn	Fracture
C.	Bite	Burn
D.	Shock	Bite

19. Refer to the given picture of Aman. Aman should go to the _______.

A. Bank

B. Post office

C. Hospital

D. Library

20. Who among the following children is/are likely to get hurt?

Sheena is playing around the swimming pool.
Sameer is walking on the footpath.
Amaira is putting her hands out of the window of a moving car.

A. Sheena only B. Sameer only

C. Amaira only D. Sheena and Amaira only

21. Which of the following statements about the Moon is correct?

A. The Moon does not have its own light.

B. The Moon has air and water on it.

C. The Moon reflects Earth's light.

D. Rotation of the Moon gives rise to day and night on Earth.

SPACE FOR ROUGH WORK

22. Unscramble the following to find out the name of a deep hole dug to get underground water.

A. ATKN　　B. UKTCBE　　C. MAD　　D. ELWL

---

23. Which of the following activities can be done with the help of air?

A. Blowing up a balloon　　B. Washing dishes
C. Washing clothes　　D. Mopping the floor

---

24. Match column I with column II and select the correct option.

	Column I		**Column II**
(a)	I give you heat and light.	1.	Earth
(b)	I go around the Sun. You live on me.	2.	Star
(c)	I appear to change my shape every day. You see me in the sky at night.	3.	Sun
		4.	Moon

A. (a)-2, (b)-3, (c)-4　　B. (a)-3, (b)-1, (c)-4
C. (a)-4, (b)-2, (c)-1　　D. (a)-3, (b)-1, (c)-2

---

25. Select the suitable heading for group X and group Y.

Group X
Cow, Horse, Sheep

Group Y
Dog, Cat, Rabbit

	X	Y
A.	Pet animals	Farm animals
B.	Domestic animals	Farm animals
C.	Domestic animals	Wild animals
D.	Farm animals	Pet animals

---

26. Deepika's sister's son is her _________.

A. Cousin　　B. Nephew　　C. Niece　　D. Brother

---

27. The weather forecast of a day during a particular season is shown in the given picture. We should wear _________ on this day.

A. Silk saree　　B. Sweater
C. Cotton frock　　D. Shorts

---

28. Which among the following has more air?

A. 　　B. 　　C. 　　D. 

SPACE FOR ROUGH WORK

29. Select the correct statement.

A. The Sun shines brightly on rainy days.
B. It gets hot when the snow falls.
C. It is very cold in the spring season.
D. The trees shed their leaves in autumn.

---

30. Ritvik was drinking hot chocolate on a winter morning. He observed 'X' over the cup. What is 'X'?

A. Smoke
B. Water droplets
C. Water vapour
D. Ice crystals

ACHIEVERS SECTION

31. Four seeds (P, Q, R and S) of the same plant are sown in four different pots. Each of the pots is treated differently as shown in the table.

Which of these seeds will be able to germinate?

A. Seed Q only
B. Seed R only
C. Both seeds R and S
D. Both seeds P and R

Seed	Air	Water	Sunlight
P	×	✓	×
Q	✓	✓	✓
R	✓	×	✓
S	✓	✓	×

---

32. Binny did a study on two animals X and Y. At the end of her study, she made the observations as shown in the given table.

Select the option that correctly identifies animals X and Y?

	Animal X	Animal Y
A.	Bear	Snake
B.	Butterfly	Frog
C.	Lion	Crow
D.	Horse	Mosquito

Observations	Animal X	Animal Y
Animal makes its own home	×	✓
Animal lays eggs	×	✓
Animal eats only other animals	✓	×

---

33. Aarav made a list of ways to save water as given here.

1. Take bath from shower rather than from bucket or tub.
2. Turn off the tap while brushing your teeth.
3. Use a bucket of water and sponge to clean the car.
4. Prefer washing fruits and vegetables in running water instead of a bowl of water.
5. Use watering can to water the plants.

Which of these ways is/are INCORRECT?

A. 3 only
B. 2, 4 and 5 only
C. 1 and 5 only
D. 1 and 4 only

SPACE FOR ROUGH WORK

Direction (Q.No. 34 and 35) : Refer to the given word grid and answer the following questions.

M	H	S	O	L	P	N	B
A	O	G	A	B	S	O	C
T	S	O	S	A	H	H	A
C	P	G	C	N	A	O	P
H	I	G	H	D	M	R	D
I	T	L	X	A	P	N	C
N	A	E	T	I	O	A	E
G	L	S	F	D	O	F	G
S	C	I	S	S	O	R	S
O	I	N	T	M	E	N	T

34. Few objects are hidden in the given word grid. How many of them are found in a first aid box?

A 2 B. 3

C. 5 D. 4

35. The meaning of which of the following road signs is hidden in the given word grid?

A. 

B. 

C. 

D. 

SCIENCE OLYMPIAD FOUNDATION
National Office: Plot 99, First Floor, Sector 44 Institutional area, Gurugram -122 003 (HR) India
Email: info@sofworld.org | Website: www.sofworld.org
Regd. Office: 406, Taj Apt., Ring Road, New Delhi-110 029
Note: Please address all communication to the National Office only.

Jungle Friends

21 CS Communication, Life Skills

HQ Cooperation and Collaborative Living

13 CLIMATE ACTION

15 LIFE ON LAND

17 PARTNERSHIPS FOR THE GOALS

One day, Piku, the parrot, spotted a woodcutter with an axe coming towards Jamun and Aam. She sensed danger!

All the animals wondered how to save their friends Jamun and Aam, who gave them food, shelter and shade.

The monkeys and birds hid among the leaves and the wolves hid behind the trees.

As the woodcutter came near the trees, the monkeys jumped on the woodcutter, the birds pecked him and the wolves started howling.

The woodcutter was frightened to see this. He understood that the trees and animals need each other. He promised, he would never cut trees.
Jamun and Aam thanked the animals for saving their lives.
Moral: In a jungle, plants and animals need each other.

SEE Learning (Social Emotional Ethical)

21 CS Communication, Life Skills | HQ Coexisting with Nature | 12 RESPONSIBLE CONSUMPTION AND PRODUCTION

Put a Stop to the Water Drop!

My SEE (Social Emotional Ethical) Space

A. Who do you think is right, Drithi or Aakshi? Discuss it with your classmates and put a tick (✓) in the box beside the right picture.

☐

☐

B. Why should we not waste water? Write the answer in the space provided below.

____

____

____

____

C. With your classmates, discuss various ways to save water. Write simple tips to be followed by everyone in our everyday life. Discuss how you can encourage your family members and friends to save water.

____

____

____

____

21 CS Creativity and Innovation AI EL

Earth Fair: Make a Leaf Sunflower Pot

Go on a nature walk with an elder and collect leaves from a park or a garden. Do not pluck leaves from trees and collect only fallen leaves. Try making a leaf sunflower pot.

All You Need Is... Long pointy leaves, yellow water colour, paint brush, brown coloured paper, scissors, glue, green paper straw, adhesive tape and a small pot filled with pebbles

Note: *Do not use scissors yourself. Take the help of an elder while cutting.*

Let's Start!

1. Use a paint brush to paint the leaves yellow in colour and let them dry.

2. With the help of an elder, cut two circles from brown coloured paper.

3. Apply glue on the brown circle and stick leaves onto it, all around.

4. Now, apply glue on the first layer of leaves and stick another layer of leaves over the first layer.

5. Add glue and stick on another brown circle over the leaves. Let the glue dry for a while.

6. Now, attach a green paper straw with some adhesive tape.

7. Place this leaf sunflower craft in a pot filled with pebbles. Your leaf sunflower pot is ready!

Do It Yourself!

With the help of an elder, make a leaf lantern. Write the things that you need and the steps of its construction. Draw or paste the pictures of the steps involved in the space provided.

A lantern is a lamp with a handle on top so that you can carry it.

All I Need Is: ____________________

____

____

____

Let's Start: ____________________

____

____

____

____

____

____

____

____

____

____

____

____

____

____

____

____

____

____

____

Eminent Personalities

Mahatma Gandhi

The Father of the nation

Saikhom Mirabai Chanu

Silver medalist at the Tokyo Olympics 2020 in weightlifting

Rabindranath Tagore

The first Nobel Prize winner from India

Sunderlal Bahuguna

The Chipko Movement leader

Sarojini Naidu

The Nightingale of India

Lovlina Borgohain

Bronze medalist at the Tokyo Olympics 2020 in boxing